The Last Laugh

A Collection of Satire

(Original title: *Cutlass & Rapier*)

Edited by
George Hillocks, Jr.
University of Chicago

SCHOLASTIC BOOK SERVICES
New York Toronto London Auckland Sydney Tokyo

Copyright © 1974 by Scholastic Magazines, Inc.
All rights reserved. Published by Scholastic Book Services,
a division of Scholastic Magazines, Inc.

1st printing   October 1974

Printed in the U. S. A.

For reprint permission, grateful acknowledgment is made to:

Broadside Press for "The Idiot" by Dudley Randall from CITIES BURNING.

Art Buchwald for "The Grown-up Problem," copyright © 1970 by Art Buchwald.

Calder and Boyars, London, for British Commonwealth rights to "The Leader" by Eugene Ionesco from vol. 4 of THE PLAYS OF EUGENE IONESCO.

Jonathan Cape Ltd., 30 Bedford Square, London, for British Commonwealth rights to "All Watched Over by Machines of Loving Grace" by Richard Brautigan from THE PILL VERSUS THE SPRINGHILL MINE DISASTER, an excerpt from Babbit by Sinclair Lewis, and an excerpt from CATCH-22 by Joseph Heller.

Collins, Knowlton-Wing, Inc., for "Symptoms of Love" by Robert Graves, copyright © 1958, 1961 by Robert Graves.

Darien House, Inc. for one poster from PROP ART, a book containing over 1,000 Contemporary Political Posters, edited by Gary Yanker. © Personality Posters 1969. Published by Darien House, Inc., and distributed by New York Graphic Society, Inc., Greenwich, CT 06830. © 1972 Gary Yanker.

Delacorte Press for "All Watched Over by Machines of Loving Grace" by Richard Brautigan from THE PILL VERSUS THE SPRINGHILL MINE DISASTER, copyright © 1968 by Richard Brautigan. A Seymour Lawrence Book.

Dodd Mead & Company, Inc., for an excerpt from TONO-BUNGAY by H. G. Wells, copyright 1908, 1936 by H. G. Wells.

Doubleday & Company, Inc., for "a spider and a fly" and "warty bliggens, the toad" by Don Marquis from THE LIVES AND TIMES OF ARCHIE AND MEHITABEL, text copyright 1930 by Doubleday & Company, Inc.

Mari Evans for "Status Symbol" from I AM A BLACK WOMAN published by William Morrow Co., 1970.

Faber and Faber Ltd. for British Commonwealth rights to "The Unknown Citizen" by W. H. Auden from COLLECTED SHORTER POEMS 1927-1957.

Contents

Introduction

Satire is a weapon. The satirist uses it to attack the vices and follies he sees in human behavior. His satire usually states or implies some standard for ideal human behavior. And he hopes that, because of his satire, people will look at themselves in a new light and change their foolish ways.

In his attack, the satirist can wield his pen as he might a cutlass, hacking and hewing his victims to pieces. Or he can wield his pen more delicately, as he would a rapier, piercing directly to the heart of his victim.

1.
Limited Vision

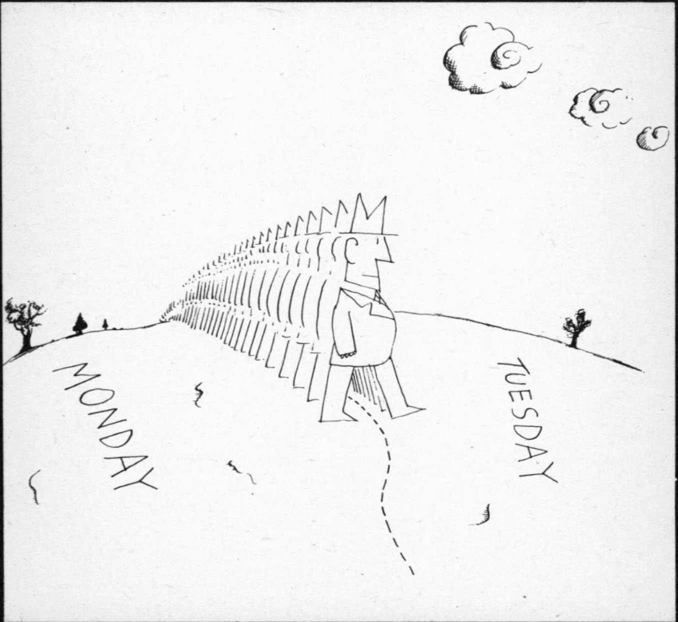
MONDAY
TUESDAY

Griffy the Cooper

The cooper should know about tubs.
But I learned about life as well,
And you who loiter around these graves
Think you know life.
You think your eye sweeps about a wide horizon,
    perhaps,
In truth you are only looking around the interior of
    your tub.
You cannot lift yourself to its rim
And see the outer world of things,
And at the same time see yourself.
You are submerged in the tub of yourself—
Taboos and rules and appearances,
Are the staves of your tub.
Break them and dispel the witchcraft
Of thinking your tub is life!
And that you know life!

Edgar Lee Masters

The Pig

by Ivan Krilof

A pig once made its way into the courtyard of a lordly mansion, sauntered at its will around the stables and the kitchen, wallowed in the mud, and then returned home from its visit a thorough pig.

"Well, Kavronya, what have you seen?" said the swineherd to the pig. "They do say that there is nothing but diamonds and gold in rich people's houses, and that each thing there is richer than the last."

"I assure you they talk nonsense," grunted Kavronya. "I saw no riches at all—nothing but dirt and offal; and yet you may suppose I didn't spare my snout, for I dug up the whole of the backyard."

warty bliggens, the toad

i met a toad
the other day by the name
of warty bliggens
he was sitting under
a toadstool
feeling contented
he explained that when the cosmos
was created
that toadstool was especially
planned for his personal
shelter from sun and rain
thought out and prepared
for him

do not tell me
said warty bliggens
that there is not a purpose
in the universe
the thought is blasphemy

a little more
conversation revealed
that warty bliggens
considers himself to be
the center of the said
universe
the earth exists
to grow toadstools for him
to sit under
the sun to give him light
by day and the moon
and wheeling constellations
to make beautiful
the night for the sake of
warty bliggens

to what act of yours
do you impute
this interest on the part
of the creator
of the universe
i asked him
why is it that you
are so greatly favored

ask rather
said warty bliggens
what the universe
has done to deserve me
if i were a
human being i would
not laugh
too complacently
at poor warty bliggens
for similar
absurdities
have only too often
lodged in the crinkles
of the human cerebrum
                archy

Don Marquis

15

The Ox and the Frog

by Aesop

An ox, browsing in a field, happened to set his foot down among some young frogs, and squashed one of them to death. The rest hopped off in terror to tell their mother of the catastrophe. The beast that did it, they added, was the most enormous creature they had ever seen. "Was it this big?" asked the old frog, swelling and puffing up her speckled green belly. "Oh, bigger by a vast deal," said they. "Was it so big?" demanded she, distending herself still more. "Oh, Mamma," they replied, "if you were to burst you would never be so big." The old frog paid no attention; she took a tremendous breath, and swelled herself till her eyes bulged. "Was it," she wheezed, "so b——" but at that moment she did indeed burst.

comforting thoughts

a fish who had
swallowed an angle worm
found all too late
that a hook was nesting
in its midst ah me
said the poor fish
i am the most luckless
creature in the world
had you not pointed
that out said the worm
i might have supposed
myself a trifle
unfortunate
cheer up you two said
the fisherman jovially
the first two minutes
of that hook are always
the worst you must
cultivate a philosophic
state of mind
boss there is always
a comforting thought
in time of trouble when
it is not our trouble
                    archy

Don Marquis

The Very Proper Gander

by James Thurber

Not so very long ago there was a very fine gander. He was strong and smooth and beautiful and he spent most of his time singing to his wife and children. One day somebody who saw him strutting up and down in his yard and singing remarked, "There is a very proper gander." An old hen overheard this and told her husband about it that night in the roost. "They said something about propaganda," she said. "I have always suspected that," said the rooster, and he went around the barnyard the next day telling everybody that the very fine gander was a dangerous bird, more than likely a hawk in gander's clothing. A small brown hen remembered a time when at a great distance she had seen the gander talking with some hawks in the forest. "They were up to no good," she said. A duck remembered that the gander had once told him he did not believe in anything. "He said he hated the flag too," said the duck. A guinea hen recalled that she had once seen somebody who looked very much like the gander throw something that looked a great deal like a bomb. Finally everybody snatched up sticks and stones and descended on the gander's house. He was strutting in his front yard, singing to his children and his wife. "There he is!" everybody cried. "Hawk-lover!" "Unbeliever!" "Flag-hater!" "Bomb-thrower!" So they set upon him and drove him out of the country.

Moral: Anybody who you or your wife thinks is going to overthrow the government by violence must be driven out of the country.

Mrs. Packletide's Tiger

by Saki

It was Mrs. Packletide's pleasure and intention that she should shoot a tiger. Not that the lust to kill had suddenly descended on her, or that she felt that she would leave India safer and more wholesome than she had found it, with one fraction less of wild beast per million of inhabitants. The compelling motive for her sudden deviation toward the footsteps of Nimrod was the fact that Loona Bimberton had recently been carried 11 miles in an airplane by an Algerian aviator, and talked of nothing else; only a personally procured tiger skin and a heavy harvest of press photographs could successfully counter that sort of thing. Mrs. Packletide had already arranged in her mind the lunch she would give at her house in Curzon Street, ostensibly in Loona Bimberton's honor, with a tiger-skin rug occupying most of the foreground and all of the conversation. She had also already designed in her mind the tiger-claw brooch that she was going to give Loona Bimberton on her next birthday. In a world that is supposed to be chiefly swayed by hunger and by love, Mrs. Packletide was an exception; her movements and motives were largely governed by dislike of Loona Bimberton.

Circumstances proved propitious. Mrs. Packletide had offered a thousand rupees for the opportunity of shooting a tiger without over-much risk or exertion, and it so happened that a neighboring village could boast of being the favored rendezvous of an animal of respectable antecedents, which had been driven by the increasing infirmities of age to abandon game-killing and confine its appetite to the smaller domestic animals. The prospect of earning the thousand rupees had stimulated the sporting and commercial instinct of the villagers; children were posted night and day on the outskirts of the local jungle to head the tiger back in the unlikely event of his attempting to roam away to fresh hunting grounds, and the cheaper kinds of goats were left about with elaborate carelessness to keep him satisfied with his present quarters. The one great anxiety was lest he should die of old age before the date appointed for the memsahib's shoot. Mothers carrying their babies home through the jungle after the day's work in the fields hushed their singing lest they might curtail the restful sleep of the venerable herd robber.

The great night duly arrived, moonlit and cloudless. A platform had been constructed in a comfortable and conveniently placed tree, and thereon crouched Mrs. Packletide and her paid companion, Miss Mebbin. A goat, gifted with a particularly persistent bleat, such as even a partially deaf tiger might be reasonably expected to hear on a still night, was tethered at the correct distance. With an accurately sighted rifle and a thumbnail pack of patience cards the sportswoman awaited the coming of the quarry.

"I suppose we are in some danger?" said Miss Mebbin.

She was not actually nervous about the wild beast, but she had a morbid dread of performing an atom more service than she had been paid for.

"Nonsense," said Mrs. Packletide; "it's a very old tiger. It couldn't spring up here even if it wanted to."

"If it's an old tiger I think you ought to get it cheaper. A thousand rupees is a lot of money."

Louisa Mebbin adopted a protective elder-sister attitude toward money in general, irrespective of nationality or denomination. Her energetic intervention had saved many a rouble from dissipating itself in tips in some Moscow hotel, and francs and centimes clung to her instinctively under circumstances which would have driven them headlong from less sympathetic hands. Her speculations as to the market depreciation of tiger remnants were cut short by the appearance on the scene of the animal itself. As soon as it caught sight of the tethered goat it lay flat on the earth, seemingly less from a desire to take advantage of all available cover than for the purpose of snatching a short rest before commencing the grand attack.

"I believe it's ill," said Louisa Mebbin, loudly in Hindustani, for the benefit of the village headman, who was in ambush in a neighboring tree.

"Hush!" said Mrs. Packletide, and at that moment the tiger commenced ambling toward his victim.

"Now, now!" urged Miss Mebbin with some excitement; "if he doesn't touch the goat we needn't pay for it." (The bait was an extra.)

The rifle flashed out with a loud report, and the great tawny beast sprang to one side and then rolled over in the stillness of death. In a moment a crowd of excited natives had swarmed on to the scene, and their shouting speedily carried the glad news to the village, where a thumping of tom-toms took up the chorus of triumph. And their triumph and rejoicing found a ready echo in the heart of Mrs. Packletide; already that luncheon party in Curzon Street seemed immeasurably nearer.

It was Louisa Mebbin who drew attention to the fact that the goat was in death throes from a mortal bullet wound, while no trace of the rifle's deadly work could be found on the tiger. Evidently the wrong animal had been hit, and the beast of prey had succumbed to heart failure, caused by the sudden report of the rifle, accelerated by senile decay. Mrs. Packletide was pardonably annoyed at the discovery; but, at any rate, she was the possessor of a dead tiger, and the villagers, anxious for their thousand rupees, gladly connived at the fiction that she had shot the beast. And Miss Mebbin was a paid companion. Therefore did Mrs. Packletide face the cameras with a light heart, and her pictured fame reached from the pages of the *Texas Weekly Snapshot* to the illustrated Monday supplement of the *Novoe Vremya*. As for Loona Bimberton, she refused to look at an illustrated paper for weeks, and her letter of thanks for the gift of a tiger-claw brooch was a model of repressed emotions. The luncheon party she declined; there are limits beyond which repressed emotions become dangerous.

From Curzon Street the tiger-skin rug traveled down to the Manor House, and was duly inspected and admired by the county, and it seemed a fitting and appropriate thing when Mrs. Packletide went to the County Costume Ball in the character of Diana. She refused to fall in, however, with Clovis' tempting suggestion of a primeval dance party, at which everyone should wear the skins of beasts they had recently slain. "I should be in rather a Baby Bunting condition," confessed Clovis, "with a miserable rabbit skin or two to wrap up in, but then," he added, with a rather malicious glance at Diana's proportions, "my figure is quite as good as that Russian dancing boy's."

"How amused everyone would be if they knew what really happened," said Louisa Mebbin a few days after the ball.

"What do you mean?" asked Mrs. Packletide quickly.

"How you shot the goat and frightened the tiger to death," said Miss Mebbin, with her disagreeably pleasant laugh.

"No one would believe it," said Mrs. Packletide, her face changing color as rapidly as though it were going through a book of patterns before post time.

"Loona Bimberton would," said Miss Mebbin. Mrs. Packletide's face settled on an unbecoming shade of greenish white.

"You surely wouldn't give me away?" she asked.

"I've seen a weekend cottage near Dorking that I should rather like to buy," said Miss Mebbin with seeming irrelevance. "Six hundred and eighty, freehold. Quite a bargain, only I don't happen to have the money."

Louisa Mebbin's pretty weekend cottage, christened by her "Les Fauves," and gay in summertime with its garden borders of tiger lilies, is the wonder and admiration of her friends.

"It is a marvel how Louisa manages to do it," is the general verdict.

Mrs. Packletide indulges in no more big-game shooting.

"The incidental expenses are so heavy," she confides to inquiring friends.

Photo courtesy The British Travel Association

In Westminster Abbey

Let me take this other glove off
   As the *vox humana*[1] swells,
And the beauteous fields of Eden
   Bask beneath the Abbey bells.
Here, where England's statesmen lie,
Listen to a lady's cry.

Gracious Lord, oh bomb the Germans.
   Spare their women for Thy Sake,
And if that is not too easy
   We will pardon Thy Mistake.
But, gracious Lord, whate'er shall be,
Don't let anyone bomb me.

[1] An organ stop that makes tones similar to those of the human voice.

Keep our Empire undismembered
    Guide our Forces by Thy Hand,
Gallant Blacks from far Jamaica,
    Honduras, and Togoland;
Protect them Lord in all their fights,
And, even more, protect the whites.

Think of what our Nation stands for,
    Books from Boots'[2] and country lanes,
Free speech, free passes, class distinction,
    Democracy, and proper drains.
Lord, put beneath Thy special care
One-eighty-nine Cadogan Square.

Although dear Lord I am a sinner,
    I have done no major crime;
Now I'll come to Evening Service
    Whensoever I have time.
So, Lord, reserve for me a crown,
And do not let my shares go down.

I will labor for Thy Kingdom,
    Help our lads to win the war,
Send white feathers to the cowards
    Join the Women's Army Corps,
Then wash the Steps around Thy Throne
In the Eternal Safety Zone.

Now I feel a little better,
    What a treat to hear Thy Word,
Where the bones of leading statesmen,
    Have so often been interr'd.
And now, dear Lord, I cannot wait
Because I have a luncheon date.

                    John Betjeman

[2] A famous pharmacy which includes a rental library.

26

Was a Man

Was a man, was a two-
faced man, pretended
he wasn't who he was,
who, in a men's room,
faced his hung-over
face in a mirror hung
over the towel rack.
The mirror was cracked.
Shaving close in that
looking glass, he nicked
his throat, bled blue
blood, grabbed a new
towel to patch the wrong
scratch, knocked off
the mirror and, facing
himself, almost intact,
in final terror hung
the wrong face back.

Philip Booth

Miniver Cheevy

Miniver Cheevy, child of scorn,
   Grew lean while he assailed the seasons;
He wept that he was ever born,
   And he had reasons.

Miniver loved the days of old
   When swords were bright and steeds were
   prancing;
The vision of a warrior bold
   Would set him dancing.

Miniver sighed for what was not,
   And dreamed, and rested from his labors;
He dreamed of Thebes and Camelot,
   And Priam's neighbors.

Miniver mourned the ripe renown
   That made so many a name so fragrant;
He mourned Romance, now on the town,
   And Art, a vagrant.

Miniver loved the Medici,
  Albeit he had never seen one;
He would have sinned incessantly
  Could he have been one.

Miniver cursed the commonplace
  And eyed a khaki suit with loathing;
He missed the medieval grace
  Of iron clothing.

Miniver scorned the gold he sought,
  But sore annoyed was he without it;
Miniver thought, and thought, and thought
  And thought about it.

Miniver Cheevy, born too late,
  Scratched his head and kept on thinking
Miniver coughed, and called it fate,
  And kept on drinking.

Edwin Arlington Robinson

The Grown-up Problem by Art Buchwald

There has been so much discussion about teenage problems that the grown-up problem is practically being ignored. And yet if you pick up a newspaper, you realize grown-ups are responsible for some of the most serious problems this country has ever faced.

For example, 60 percent of all crime in the United States is committed by grown-ups.

The birth rate among grown-up women is four times that of teenagers.

The divorce rate is double.

The purchasing power of grown-ups almost exceeds that of teenagers.

Grown-ups are responsible for more daytime accidents than any other age group.

The source of these statistics is sociology professor Heinrich Applebaum, B.A., M.S., LL.D., Y.E.H., Y.E.H, Y.E.H., who told me in an exclusive interview that his studies showed grown-ups were drifting farther away from society all the time.

"The average grown-up," Professor Applebaum said, "feels his children don't understand him. The more time he spends with them, the less they communicate with him. So the adult feels isolated, insecure, and misunderstood. In defense he seeks out other grown-ups who feel the same way he does. Pretty soon they form gangs, go to the theater together, hold cocktail parties and dances, and before you know it you have a complete breakdown of the family."

"Why do you think grown-ups are constantly

rebelling against their children, Professor?"

"I guess it's an age-old problem. You have parents wanting to break away and yet not having the nerve to cut the ties completely. Grown-ups are afraid to stand up to their children, so they rebel against society instead."

"Do you think teenagers could in some way be responsible for the behavior of their parents?"

"I definitely do," the Professor said. "Grown-ups try to emulate teenagers. They want to do exactly what teenagers do, which is to drink, smoke, and drive fast cars. If teenagers didn't do these things, their parents wouldn't. For every bad adult in America, I'm sure you'll find a bad teenager somewhere in the background."

"Where do you think the trouble starts?"

"In the home. Teenagers are too rough on their parents. They're always criticizing them for listening to Frank Sinatra records and reading *Holiday* magazine. Teenagers don't have any patience with their mothers and fathers. They can't understand why their parents like Doris Day and Rock Hudson movies or what they see in Cary Grant. If teenagers spent more time with grown-ups and tried to understand them, I don't think you'd have half the trouble that you have in the United States today."

"Do you mean teenagers should spend more time at home with their parents?"

"Of course. Grown-ups need security. They want to know where their children are. They want the feeling they belong. Only teenagers can give grown-ups this feeling."

"Professor, have you found any homes where grown-ups are leading healthy, normal, secure lives, thanks to the attention they've received from their loving teenage children?"

"We haven't yet. But we've been looking only a year. These surveys take time."

The Purist

I give you now Professor Twist,
A conscientious scientist.
Trustees exclaimed, "He never bungles!"
And sent him off to distant jungles.
Camped on a tropic riverside,
One day he missed his loving bride.
She had, the guide informed him later,
Been eaten by an alligator.
Professor Twist could not but smile.
"You mean," he said, "a crocodile."

Ogden Nash

We Real Cool

The Pool Players
Seven at the Golden Shovel.

We real cool. We
Left school. We

Lurk late. We
Strike straight. We

Sing sin. We
Thin gin. We

Jazz June. We
Die soon.

Gwendolyn Brooks

Two Friends

I have something to tell you.
I'm listening.
I'm dying.
I'm sorry to hear.
I'm growing old.
It's terrible.
It is, I thought you should know.
Of course and I'm sorry. Keep in touch.
I will and you too.
And let me know what's new.
Certainly, though it can't be much.
And stay well.
And you too.
And go slow.
And you too.

David Ignatow

The Idiot

"That cop was powerful mean.
First he called me, 'Black boy.'
Then he punched me in the face
and drug me by the collar to a wall
and made me lean against it with my hands spread
while he searched me,
and all the time he searched me
he kicked me and cuffed me and cussed me.

"I was mad enough
to lay him out,
and would've did it, only
I didn't want to hurt his feelings,
and lose the goodwill
of the good white folks downtown,
who hired him."

Dudley Randall

The Still Alarm

by George S. Kaufman

CHARACTERS

ED
BOB
BELLBOY
FIRST FIREMAN
SECOND FIREMAN

SCENE: *A hotel bedroom*

VITAL NOTE: *It is important that the entire play should be acted calmly and politely, in the manner of an English drawing-room comedy. No actor ever raises his voice; every line must be read as though it were an invitation to a cup of tea. If this direction is disregarded, the play has no point at all. The scene is a hotel bedroom. Two windows rear; door to the hall at the right, chair R.C. Bed between windows. Phone stand R., downstage end of bed. Dresser L.U. corner. Another door at left. Small table and chairs downstage L.C.*

ED *and* BOB *are on the stage.* ED *is getting into his overcoat as the curtain rises. Both are at R. door.*

ED: Well, Bob, it's certainly been nice to see you again.

BOB: It was nice to see *you*.

ED: You come to town so seldom, I hardly ever get the chance to —

BOB: Well, you know how it is. A business trip is always more or less of a bore.

ED: Next time you've got to come out to the house.

BOB: I want to come out. I just had to stick around the hotel this trip.

ED: Oh, I understand. Well, give my best to Edith.

BOB (*remembering something*): Oh, I say, Ed. Wait a minute.

ED: What's the matter?

BOB: I knew I wanted to show you something. (*Crosses L. to table. Gets roll of blueprints from drawer.*) Did you know I'm going to build?

ED (*follows to R. of table*): A house?

BOB: You bet it's a house! (*Knock on R. door.*) Come in! (*Spreads plans.*) I just got these yesterday.

ED (*sits*): Well, that's fine! (*The knock is repeated — louder. Both men now give full attention to the door.*)

BOB: Come! Come in!

BELLBOY (*enters*): Mr. Barclay?

BOB: Well?

BELLBOY: I've a message from the clerk, sir. For Mr. Barclay personally.

BOB (*crosses to boy*): I'm Mr. Barclay. What is the message?

BELLBOY: The hotel is on fire, sir.

BOB: What's that?

BELLBOY: The hotel is on fire.

ED: This hotel?

BELLBOY: Yes, sir.

BOB: Well — is it bad?

BELLBOY: It looks pretty bad, sir.

ED: You mean it's going to burn down?

BELLBOY: We think so — yes, sir.

BOB (*a low whistle of surprise*): Well! We'd better leave.

BELLBOY: Yes, sir.

BOB: Going to burn down, huh?

BELLBOY: Yes, sir. If you'll step to the window you'll see.

(BOB *goes to* R. *window.*)

BOB: Yes, that is pretty bad. H'm. (*To* ED.) I say, you really ought to see this —

ED (*crosses up to* R. *window — peering out*): It's reached the floor right underneath.

BELLBOY: Yes, sir. The lower part of the hotel is about gone, sir.

BOB (*still looking out — looks up*): Still all right up above, though. (*Turns to boy.*) Have they notified the Fire Department?

BELLBOY: I wouldn't know, sir. I'm only the bell-boy.

BOB: Well, that's the thing to do, obviously — (*Nods head to each one as if the previous line was a bright idea.*) — notify the Fire department. Just call them up, give them the name of the hotel —

ED: Wait a minute. I can do better than that for you. (*To the boy.*) Ring through to the Chief, and tell him that Ed Jamison told you to telephone him. (*To* BOB.) We went to school together, you know.

BOB: That's fine. (*To the boy.*) Now, get that right. Tell the Chief that Mr. Jamison said to ring him.

ED: *Ed* Jamison.

BOB: Yes, *Ed* Jamison.

BELLBOY: Yes, sir. (*Turns to go.*)

BOB: Oh! Boy! (*Pulls out handful of change; picks*

out a coin.) Here you are.

BELLBOY: Thank you, sir. (*Exit* BELLBOY. ED *sits R. of table, lights cigarette and throws match downstage, then steps on it. There is a moment's pause.*)

BOB: Well! (*Crosses and looks out L. window.*) Say, we'll have to get out of here pretty soon.

ED (*going to window*): How is it — no better?

BOB: Worse, if anything. It'll be up here in a few moments.

ED: What floor *is* this?

BOB: Eleventh.

ED: Eleven. We couldn't jump, then.

BOB: Oh, no. You never could jump. (*Comes away from window to dresser.*) Well, I've got to get my things together. (*Pulls out suitcase.*)

ED (*smoothing out the plans*): Who made these for you?

BOB: A fellow here — Rawlins. (*Turns a shirt in his hand.*) I ought to call one of the other hotels for a room.

ED: Oh, you can get in.

BOB: They're pretty crowded. (*Feels something on the sole of his foot; inspects it.*) Say, the floor's getting hot.

ED: I know it. It's getting stuffy in the room too. Phew! (*He looks around, then goes to the phone.*) Hello — Ice water in 11-18. (*Crosses to R. of table.*)

BOB (*at bed*): That's the stuff. (*Packs.*) You know, if I move to another hotel I'll never get my mail. Everybody thinks that I'm stopping here.

ED (*studying the plans*): Say, this isn't bad.

BOB (*eagerly*): Do you like it? (*Remembers his plight.*) Suppose I go to another hotel and there's a fire there too!

39

ED: You've got to take *some* chance.

BOB: I know, but here I'm sure. (*Phone rings.*) Oh, answer that, will you, Ed? (*To dresser and back.*)

ED (*crosses to phone*): Sure. (*At phone.*) Hello — Oh, that's good. Fine. What? — Oh! Well, wait a minute. (*To* BOB.) The firemen are downstairs and some of them want to come up to this room.

BOB: Tell them, of course.

ED (*at phone*): All right. Come right up. (*Hangs up, crosses and sits R. of table.*) Now we'll get some action.

BOB (*looks out of window L.*): Say, there's an awful crowd of people on the street.

ED (*absently, as he pores over the plans*): Maybe there's been some kind of accident.

BOB (*peering out, suitcase in hand*): No. More likely they heard about the fire. (*A knock at the door R.*) Come in.

BELLBOY (*enters*): I beg pardon, Mr. Barclay, the firemen have arrived.

BOB: Show them in. (*Crosses to R. The door opens. In the doorway appear two* FIREMEN *in full regalia. The* FIRST FIREMAN *carries a hose and a rubber coat; the* SECOND *has a violin case,* R.C.)

FIRST FIREMAN (*enters R. Very apologetically*): Mr. Barclay?

BOB: I'm Mr. Barclay.

FIRST FIREMAN: We're the firemen, Mr. Barclay. (*They remove their hats.*)

BOB: How de do?

ED: How de do?

BOB: A great pleasure, I assure you. Really must apologize for the condition of this room, but —

FIRST FIREMAN: Oh, that's all right. I know how it is at home.

BOB: May I present a friend of mine, Mr. Ed Jamison —

FIRST FIREMAN: How are you?

ED: How are you, boys? (SECOND FIREMAN *nods.*) I know your Chief.

FIRST FIREMAN: Oh, is that so? He knows the Chief — dear old Chiefie. (SECOND FIREMAN *giggles.*)

BOB (*embarrassed*): Well, I guess you boys want to get to work, don't you?

FIRST FIREMAN: Well, if you don't mind. We would like to spray around a little bit.

BOB: May I help you?

FIRST FIREMAN: Yes, if you please. (BOB *helps him into his rubber coat. At the same time the* SECOND FIREMAN, *without a word, lays the violin case on the bed, opens it, takes out the violin, and begins tuning it.*)

BOB (*watching him*): I don't think I understand.

FIRST FIREMAN: Well, you see, Sid doesn't get much chance to practice at home. Sometimes, at a fire, while we're waiting for a wall to fall or something, why, a fireman doesn't really have anything to do, and personally I like to see him improve himself symphonically. I hope you don't resent it. You're not antisymphonic?

BOB: Of course not — (BOB *and* ED *nod understandingly; the* SECOND FIREMAN *is now waxing the bow.*)

FIRST FIREMAN: Well, if you'll excuse me — (*To window R. Turns with decision toward the window. You feel that he is about to get down to business.*)

BOB (*crosses* L.): Charming personalities.

ED (*follows over to the window* R.): How is the fire?

FIRST FIREMAN (*feels the wall*): It's pretty bad right now. This wall will go pretty soon now, but it'll fall out that way, so it's all right. (*Peers out.*) That next room is the place to fight it from.

(*Crosses to door* L. BOB *shows ties as* ED *crosses.*)

ED (*sees ties*): Oh! Aren't those gorgeous!

FIRST FIREMAN (*to* BOB): Have you the key for this room?

BOB: Why, no. I've nothing to do with that room. I've just got this one. (*Folding a shirt as he talks.*)

ED: Oh, it's very comfortable.

FIRST FIREMAN: That's too bad, I had something up my sleeve. If I could have gotten in there. Oh, well, may I use your phone?

BOB: Please do. (*To* ED.) Do you think you might hold this? (*Indicates the hose.*)

ED: How?

FIRST FIREMAN: Just crawl under it. (*As he does that.*) Thanks. (*At phone.*) Hello. Let me have the clerk, please. (*To* SECOND FIREMAN.) Give us that little thing you played the night the Equitable Building burned down. (*Back to phone.*) Are you there? This is one of the firemen. Oh, *you* know. I'm in a room — ah — (*Looks at* BOB.)

BOB: Eleven-eighteen.

FIRST FIREMAN: Eleven-eighteen, and I want to get into the next room — Oh, goody. Will you send someone up with the key? There's no one in there? Oh, super-goody! Right away. (*Hangs up.*)

BOB: That's fine. (*To* FIREMAN.) Won't you sit down?

FIRST FIREMAN: Thanks.

ED: Have a cigar?

FIRST FIREMAN (*takes it*): Much obliged.

BOB: A light?

FIRST FIREMAN: If you please.

ED (*failing to find a match*): Bob, have you a match?

BOB (*crosses to* L.C.): I thought there were some here. (*Hands in pockets.*)

FIRST FIREMAN: Oh, never mind. (*He goes to* R.

window, leans out, and emerges with cigar lighted. BOB crosses L. to dresser; slams drawer. The SECOND FIREMAN taps violin with bow.)

FIRST FIREMAN: Mr. Barclay, I think he's ready now.

BOB *(takes chair from R. table and sits C.):* Pardon me. *(They all sit. The SECOND FIREMAN takes center of stage, with all the manner of a concert violinist. He goes into "Keep the Home Fires Burning." BOB, ED, and FIRST FIREMAN wipe brows as curtain falls.)*

CURTAIN

2.
Mechanization

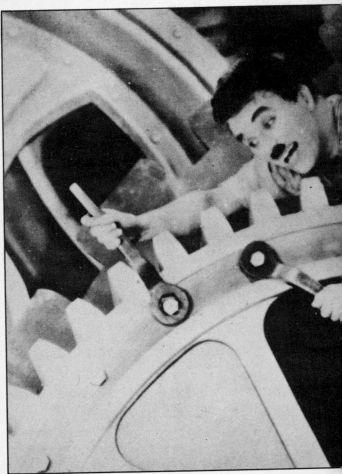

From MODERN TIMES

Little Boxes

Little boxes on the hillside,
Little boxes made of ticky tacky,
Little boxes on the hillside,
Little boxes all the same;
There's a green one and a pink one
And a blue one and a yellow one
And they're all made out of ticky tacky
And they all look just the same.

And the people in the houses
All went to the university,
Where they were put in boxes
And they came out all the same,
And there's doctors and lawyers,
And business executives,
And they're all made out ot ticky tacky
And they all look just the same.

Little boxes on the hillside,
Little boxes made of ticky tacky,
Little boxes on the hillside,
Little boxes all the same;
And the boys go into business
And marry and raise a family
In boxes made of ticky tacky
And they all look just the same.

And they all play on the golf course
And drink their martinis dry,
And they all have pretty children
And the children go to school,
And the children go to summer camp
And then to the university,
Where they are put in boxes
And they come out all the same.

Words and Music
By Malvina Reynolds

Copyright 1962 by Schroder Music Co.

The Dog and the Wolf

by Aesop

A gaunt wolf was almost dead with hunger when he happened to meet a house dog who was passing by. "Ah, Cousin," said the dog, "I knew how it would be; your irregular life will soon be the ruin of you. Why do you not work steadily as I do, and get your food regularly given to you?"

"I would have no objection," said the wolf, "if I could only get a place."

"I will easily arrange that for you," said the dog. "Come with me to my master and you shall share my work."

So the wolf and the dog went toward the town together. On the way there the wolf noticed that the hair on a certain part of the dog's neck was very much worn away, so he asked him how that had come about.

"Oh, it is nothing," said the dog. "That is only the place where the collar is put on at night to keep me chained up; it chafes a bit, but one soon gets used to it."

"Is that all?" said the wolf. "Then good-bye to you, Master Dog. I would rather starve free than be a fat slave."

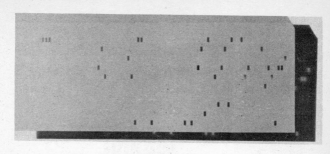

R U There?

by Constance L. Melaro

August 17

Dear Madam:

Our records show an outstanding balance of $2.98 on your account. If you have already remitted this amount, kindly disregard this notice.

THIS IS A BUSINESS MACHINE CARD
PLEASE DO NOT SPINDLE OR MUTILATE.

August 19

Gentlemen:

I do *not* have an outstanding balance. I attached a note with my payment advising you that I had been billed *twice* for the same amount: once under my first name, middle initial, and last name; and then under my two first initials and my last name. (The former is correct.) Please check your records.

Dear Madam:

Our records show a delinquent balance of $2.98 on your account. Please remit $3.40. This includes a handling charge.

THIS IS A BUSINESS MACHINE CARD.
PLEASE DO NOT SPINDLE OR MUTILATE.

Dear Machine:

You're not paying attention! I am NOT delinquent in any amount. I do *not* owe this money. I was billed TWICE for the same purchase. PLEASE look into this.

Dear Madam:

Our records show you to be delinquent for three months. Please remit the new charges plus $4.10. (This includes a handling charge.) May we have your immediate attention in this matter.

THIS IS A BUSINESS MACHINE CARD.
PLEASE DO NOT SPINDLE OR MUTILATE.

Dear Machine:

MY attention! You want MY attention! Listen here, YOU ARE WRONG!!! I DON'T owe you $4.10. CAN YOU UNDERSTAND THAT? I also DON'T owe you the new charges of $13.46. You billed ME for my MOTHER'S purchase. Please correct this statement AT ONCE!

Dear Madam:

Our records now show you to be delinquent for

50

four months in the total amount of $17.56 plus $1.87 handling charges. Please remit in full in 10 days or your account will be turned over to our Auditing Department for collection.

November 19

Dear Human Machine Programmer —
Dear ANYONE human:
   WILL YOU PLEASE TAKE YOUR HEAD OUT OF THE COMPUTER LONG ENOUGH TO READ THIS? I DON'T OWE YOU THIS MONEY!!! I DON'T OWE YOU *ANY* MONEY. *NONE.*

December 17

Dear Madam:
   Is there some question about your statement? Our records show no payment on your account since August. Please call DI 7-9601 and ask for Miss Gilbert at your earliest convenience.

DECEMBER 18
   ...Deck the halls with boughs of holly...
"Good afternoon. Carver's hopes you enjoyed its recorded program of carols. May I help you?"
   "Hello. Yes...My bill is...should I wait for a 'beep' before I talk?"
   "About your bill?"
   "Yes. Yes, it's my bill. There's..."
   Good afternoon and Merry Christmas. This is a recorded message. All our lines are in service now. If

51

you will please be patient, one of our adjusters will be with you just as soon as a line is free. Meanwhile, Carver's hopes you will enjoy its program of Christmas carols... Deck the halls with...

December 26

Dear Machine:

I tried to call you on December 18. Also the 19th, 20th, 21st, 22nd, the 23rd, and the 24th. But all I got was a recorded message and those Christmas Carols. Please, oh, please! Won't you turn me over to a human? *Any* human?

January 17

Dear Madam:

Our Credit Department has turned your delinquent account over to us for collection. Won't you please remit this amount now? We wish to cooperate with you in every way possible, but this is considerably past due. May we have your check at this time.

Very truly yours,
HENRY J. HOOPER, Auditor

January 19

Dear Mr. Hooper:

You DOLL! I refer you to letters I sent to your department, dated the 19th of August, September, October, and November, and the 26th of December, which should clarify that I owe you nothing.

February 17

Dear Madam:

According to our microfilm records, our billing

was in error. Your account is clear; you have no balance. We hope there will be no further inconvenience to you. Though this was our fault, you can help us if, in the future, you will always include your account number when ordering by mail or phone.

> Very truly yours,
> HENRY J. HOOPER, Auditor

February 19

Dear Mr. Hooper:
Thank you! Oh, thank you, thank you!

March 17

Dear Madam:
Our records show you to be delinquent in the amount of $2.98, erroneously posted last August to a nonexistent account. May we have your remittance at this time?

> THIS IS A BUSINESS MACHINE CARD.
> PLEASE DO NOT SPINDLE OR MUTILATE.

March 19

Dear Machine:
I give up. You win. Here's a check for $2.98. Enjoy yourself.

April 17

Dear Madam:
Our records show an overpayment on your part of $2.98. We are crediting this amount to your account.

> THIS IS A BUSINESS MACHINE CARD.
> PLEASE DO NOT SPINDLE OR MUTILATE.

The Unknown Citizen

(To JS/07/M/378 This Marble Monument is Erected
   by the State)
He was found by the Bureau of Statistics to be
One against whom there was no official complaint,
And all the reports on his conduct agree
That, in the modern sense of an old-fashioned word,
   he was a saint,
For in everything he did he served the Greater Com-
   munity.
Except for the War till the day he retired
He worked in a factory and never got fired,
But satisfied his employers, Fudge Motors Inc.

Yet he wasn't a scab or odd in his views,
For his Union reports that he paid his dues,
(Our report on his Union shows it was sound)
And our Social Psychology workers found
That he was popular with his mates and liked a
drink.
The press are convinced that he bought a paper every
day
And that his reactions to advertisements were normal
in every way.
Policies taken out in his name prove that he was fully
insured,
And his health card shows he was once in hospital
but left it cured.
Both Producers Research and High-Grade Living
declare
He was fully sensible to the advantages of the Install-
ment Plan
And had everything necessary to the Modern Man,
A phonograph, a radio, a car, and a frigidaire.
Our researchers into Public Opinion are content
That he held the proper opinions for the time of
year:
When there was peace, he was for peace; when there
was war, he went.
He was married and added five children to the popu-
lation,
Which our Eugenist says was the right number for a
parent of his generation,
And our teachers report that he never interfered with
their education.
Was he free? Was he happy? The question is absurd:
Had anything been wrong, we should certainly have
heard.

W. H. Auden

The Invention of New Jersey

Place a custard stand in a garden
or in place of a custard stand
   place a tumbled-down custard stand
in place of a tumbled-down custard stand
   place minature golf in a garden
   and an advertisement for miniature golf
     shaped for no apparent reason
     like an old Dutch windmill
in place of a swamp
   place a swamp

     or a pizzeria called the Tower of Pizza
      sporting a scale model
       of the Tower of Pisa
     or a water tower resembling
      a roll-on deodorant
     or a Dixie Cup factory
      with a giant metal Dixie Cup on the roof

In place of wolverines, rabbits, or melons
   place a vulcanizing plant
in place of a deer
   place an iron deer
   at a lawn furniture store
   selling iron deer
     Negro jockeys
     Bavarian gnomes
     and imitation grottoes
     with electric Infants of Prague

in place of phosphorescence
   of marshy ground at night
      place smears of rubbish fires
in place of brown water with minnows
      place brown water
         gigantic landlords
         in the doorways of apartment houses
         which look like auto showrooms
         auto showrooms which look like diners
         diners which look like motels
         motels which look like plastic chair covers
         plastic chair covers which look like
         plastic table covers which look like plastic
           bags
         the mad scientist of Secaucus
         invents a plastic cover
         to cover the lawn
         with millions of perforations
         for the grass to poke through

In place of the straight lines of grasses
   place the straight lines of gantries
in place of lights in the window
   place lighted refineries
in place of a river
   place the road like a slim pair of pants
      set to dry beside a neon frankfurter
in place of New Jersey
   place a plastic New Jersey

Jack Anderson

Paper Men To Air Hopes and Fears

The first speaker said
Fear fire. Fear furnaces
Incinerators, the city dump
The faint scratch of match.

The second speaker said
Fear water. Fear drenching rain
Drizzle, oceans, puddles, a damp
Day and the flush toilet.

The third speaker said
Fear wind. And it needn't be
A hurricane. Drafts, open
Windows, electric fans.

The fourth speaker said
Fear knives. Fear any sharp
Thing, machine, shears
Scissors, lawnmowers.

The fifth speaker said
Hope. Hope for the best
A smooth folder in a steel file.

Robert Francis

All Watched Over by Machines of Loving Grace

I like to think
      (and the sooner the better!)
of a cybernetic meadow
where mammals and computers
live together in mutually
programming harmony
like pure water
touching clear sky.

I like to think
      (right now, please!)
of a cybernetic forest,
filled with pines and electronics
where deer stroll peacefully
past computers
as if they were flowers
with spinning blossoms.

I like to think
      (it has to be!)
of a cybernetic ecology
where we are free of our labors
and joined back to nature,
returned to our mammal
brothers and sisters,
and all watched over
by machines of loving grace.

Richard Brautigan

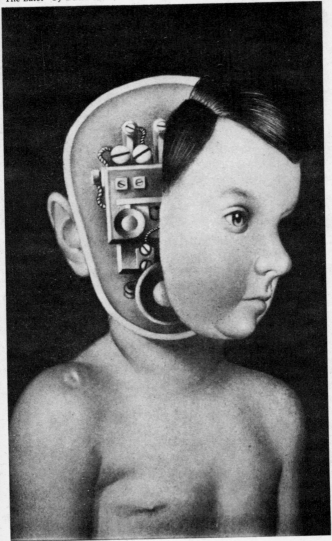

Sacre
du Printemps

by Ludwig Bemelmans

The Undersecretary of the Division of Spring of the
Ministry of the Four Seasons unrolled an ivy-green
runner on the balcony of the Ministry of Strength-
Through-Joy at the precise moment that the Undersecretary of the Ministry of Discipline and Order
placed thereon his microphone; then both listened to
the bells strike seven in the morning and opened the
door behind which stood in proper uniform, with all
buttons buttoned, the Ministers of Spring, of Discipline and Order, and of Strength-Through-Joy.
The Minister of the Four Seasons and the Minister of
Discipline and Order announced the beginning of
Spring.

Dutifully, with dispatch and promptness, there
appeared blossoms in their proper colors on all trees
in the land, buttercups growing orderly along the
brooks opened their little faces to the sun, forget-me-
nots in the forests, heather in the marshes, daisies
among the fields, and even edelweiss high up in the
mountains.

In the window boxes of the workingmen geraniums bloomed, tulips in the gardens of the civil servants of the classes 1, 2, 3, 4, and 5, and roses in the classes from 6 to 12. Above that, in classes 13 to 15, there was no need of Spring — flowers were in bloom the year round in the winter gardens of generals, bishops, directors of banks and gas factories. Heartwarming and admirable was the success with which the State and particularly the Ministry of Strength-Through-Joy, the Division of Spring of the Ministry of the Four Seasons, and the Ministry of Discipline had succeeded in the administration of all details, down to the orderly joy of the little girls, who marched out into the lovely greenery in proper white starched dresses and in battalion formation, starting at seven-thirty in the morning, the smallest in front, the tallest in back.

There the little girls stopped to sing the appropriate songs, simple *Lieder* written for the occasion. On this day there were sung: The *Lied* of the *Lindenbaum* for the linden trees, the song of the *Heidenröslein*, for the little wild rose. How good! How without problems was life ahead for the little blond girls! How provident was the Ministry of the Four Seasons and, for that matter, the Ministry of Youth, of Motherhood, and even of Love!

No one was forgotten. The railroads ran extra trains to take each and every citizen out into the Spring. And even the railroad was an example of the forethought and order of the provident State. There were first-class carriages with red plush upholstery and amber curtains; there were second-class compartments with green herringbone sailcloth; third class (a) with wooden seats, soft wood tailored to conform to the curves of the body; and third class (b) with hard wooden benches, noncomforming; and sixth-class carriages, to stand up in.

Malcontents, enemies of the government, and scoffers told of a sixth-class carriage that had no floor — just a roof and sides — in which the passengers had to run along the tracks. That, of course, was not so. Besides, there were no malcontents left.

The unsleeping vigilance of the Ministry of Justice had run all nonconformists into the ground, or successfully converted them. That is, all but one man, the Outsider, the One, by name Kratzig, Emil, who walked alone in his own disorderly path.

When all the citizens were out in the Spring, Emil Kratzig sat at home with his curtains drawn and read forbidden books; and again when all were snug at home in the Winter singing the songs of the "Oven," "Grandfather's clock, ticktock, ticktock," or "*Ich bin so gern, so gern daheim, daheim in meiner stillen Klause*," he ran around outside in the snow and whistled.

There was a long official report under K — Kratzig, Emil. But while the Political Police shadowed him, they nevertheless left him alone. They did not disturb him. "We must save him," said the Minister of Justice. "He is the last one; we may need him as an example." Besides, Emil Kratzig was an old man, and a foreigner: His maternal great-grandfather had been a Frenchman.

So Emil Kratzig lived apart and sat alone. And on the street the policeman, Umlauf, who was stationed at the City Hall square to keep him under surveillance, filled his little notebook with the discordant reports of the goings and comings of the dissenter.

The leaves in the official notebook of Policeman Umlauf, pages 48 to 55, carry the story of the sad end of the incorrigible, insubordinate Emil Kratzig....

On the sunlit morning of a green May day, when all in the city went out to look at the blossoms, take deep breaths, and sing in the new, light-flowered prints designed by the Ministry of Dress and Underwear, Kratzig, wrapped in a muffler, burdened with galoshes and heavy winter coat, fled alone to the meanest landscape he could find, a district that contained the municipal incinerators, the garbage trucks, and the street-cleaning apparatus. There he spent the day crossing and recrossing the cobblestones, with wild tirades; made free with the names of ministers, the government, the nation as a whole; and that night came home and slept with open windows. That night, of course, there was a frost, and it was this frost which took many blossoms and reached out also for the life of Emil Kratzig.

The next day Emil Kratzig was ill. A cold turned to pleurisy of the left lobar cavity, and the government doctor, who came the following day and ordered him to stay, in bed, shook his head as he left the house. But Emil Kratzig got up again, in violation of the doctor's orders, and with a high fever ran to the City Hall.

"Aha," said Policeman Umlauf, and in his notebook he remarked: "The end is near and Herr Kratzig is coming to heel."

And it looked as if at last, indeed, this misguided Kratzig had decided to mend his ways. He passed by the Bureaus of Birth, Taxation, and Marriages, and properly opened the door to the Bureau of Funerals, on the second floor. He entered the room, removed his hat, and stood quietly in the line of citizens who had business with the clerk of that department. He patiently awaited his turn with hat in hand and finally spoke his desire... to make arrangements for himself.

The clerk pushed forward a chair for Herr Kratzig. On the top of his desk was a large album. He opened it for Emil Kratzig's inspection.

The Chief Clerk appeared and pushed a platoon of underclerks away. With his own lips he blew dust from the funeral album (this album was used only in extraordinary cases); he washed his hands in the air with anticipation, patted Kratzig on the shoulder, cleared his throat, and opened the cover.

"Now this," said the Chief Clerk, "is the first-class funeral." He pointed to the first of the many pictures and recited, "The first-class funeral is composed of the wagon, first class," indicating with the rubber end of his pencil the four angels of Annunciation carved in the teakwood, who stood at the four corners of the wagon, at the rubber tires, at the betasseled curtains of black brocade.

"This wagon is drawn by six horses, with black cloaks and black plumes. They wear this silver harness. There is besides a bishop and two priests, 60 *Sängerknaben*, a band, the bells of all the churches ring, there is a salute of guns, incense, and, at the High Mass, twelve of these golden candelabra are used with scented beeswax candles. But this is not for you. It is for the classes 13 to 15 of the Civil Service."

He turned the page of the second-class funeral. "Here we have the same car, rubber tires, four horses with black cloaks, black plumes, and silver harness, three priests, but no bishop, forty *Sängerknaben*, incense, six of the first-class candelabra at the High Mass, the bells of half the churches, no guns, and, in the first-class candelabra, plain unscented candles."

Again he turned a huge page. "Now we come to the third-class funeral," he continued. "There is a different wagon, but also very nice, with one mourning angel sitting on top, cretonne curtains, two horses with nickel harness, black cloaks and plumes, two priests, no *Sängerknaben*, but a male quartet, nickel candelabra, of course no guns, but the two bells of the cemetery chapel and one priest with two apprentice priests, incense, and a very nice grade of candles, not beeswax but scented. But that is not for you either."

He shifted the weight of his body to his left foot and his voice changed. "The fourth-class funeral is somewhat plainer. We have here the wagon of the third class, one horse with cloak and plume and nickel harness, one priest, one singer, two altar boys, and incense. For the Mass, organ music and two candelabra with candles.

"The fifth-class funeral," he went on, "is here." And he turned the page. "Here is a strong solid wagon, and one horse, no cloak, no plume, but it is a black horse, an apprentice priest, and one singer, one altar boy, incense, no music at the Mass, and two wooden candelabra with used candles."

He paused.

"And finally we come to the sixth-class funeral," he said. "Here again you get the wagon of the fifth class, the black horse, an apprentice priest, no singer, one altar boy, two wooden candelabra with used substitute-wax candles, a little bell." And he turned the page to show a drawing. "And with this funeral goes a rented coffin — it saves you buying one."

A working drawing of this imaginative, melancholy piece of black carpentry was attached, also photographs showing its economical performance. It looked like any other frugal coffin, but had an ingenious device — two doors at the bottom opened when a lever was pulled. Once occupied and having been carried to its destination, the coffin opened at the bottom and the occupant was dropped into the grave. So the rented coffin could be used over and over again.

"Very simple, after all," said the clerk and, turning, he left the sentence open, because Emil Kratzig was gone.

Emil Kratzig was not seen again until the middle of the next night. Policeman Umlauf, standing in the center of the market square, saw a pale man coming toward him. The man was dressed in a long white nightshirt. On his head was a top hat. Tied to it with a piece of crepe was a black plume. In his hand he held two burning candles and he carried a shovel under his arm.

"I am Emil Kratzig," said the man. "I died last night. I am going up to the cemetery. This is a seventh-class funeral."

From BOY, GIRL, BOY, GIRL by Jules Feiffer

Copyright © 1959, 1960, 1961 by Jules Feiffer

3.The People

The Owl Who Was God

by James Thurber

Once upon a starless midnight there was an owl who sat on the branch of an oak tree. Two ground moles tried to slip quietly by, unnoticed. "You!" said the owl. "Who?" they quavered, in fear and astonishment, for they could not believe it was possible for anyone to see them in that thick darkness. "You two!" said the owl. The moles hurried away and told the other creatures of the field and forest that the owl was the greatest and wisest of all animals because he could see in the dark and because he could answer any question. "I'll see about that," said a secretary bird, and he called on the owl one night when it was again very dark. "How many claws am I holding up?" said the secretary bird. "Two," said the owl, and that was right. "Can you give me another expression for 'that is to say' or 'namely'?" asked the secretary bird. "To wit," said the owl. "Why does a lover call on his love?" asked the secretary bird. "To woo," said the owl.

The secretary bird hastened back to the other creatures and reported that the owl was indeed the great-

74

est and wisest animal in the world because he could see in the dark and because he could answer any question. "Can he see in the daytime too?" asked a red fox. "Yes," echoed a dormouse and a French poodle, "can he see in the daytime too?" All the other creatures laughed loudly at this silly question, and they set upon the red fox and his friends and drove them out of the region. Then they sent a messenger to the owl and asked him to be their leader.

When the owl appeared among the animals it was high noon and the sun was shining brightly. He walked very slowly, which gave him an appearance of great dignity, and he peered about him with large, staring eyes, which gave him an air of tremendous importance. "He's God!" screamed a Plymouth Rock hen. And the others took up the cry, "He's God!" So they followed him wherever he went and when he began to bump into things they began to bump into things too. Finally he came to a concrete highway and he started up the middle of it and all the other creatures followed him. Presently a hawk, who was acting as outrider, observed a truck coming toward them at 50 miles an hour, and he reported to the secretary bird and the secretary bird reported to the owl. "There's danger ahead," said the secreatry bird. "To wit?" said the owl. The secretary bird told him. "Aren't you afraid?" he asked. "Who?" said the owl calmly, for he could not see the truck. "He's God!" cried all the creatures again, and they were still crying, "He's God!" when the truck hit them and ran them down. Some of the animals were merely injured, but most of them, including the owl, were killed.

Moral: You can fool too many of the people too much of the time.

The Leader

by Eugene Ionesco

CHARACTERS

ANOUNCER
YOUNG LOVER
GIRL FRIEND

ADMIRER
GIRL ADMIRER
LEADER

(*Standing with his back to the public, center-stage, and with his eyes fixed on the upstage exit, the ANNOUNCER waits for the arrival of the LEADER. To right and left, riveted to the walls, two of the leader's ADMIRERS, a man and a girl, also wait for his arrival.*)

ANNOUNCER (*after a few tense moments in the same position*): There he is! There he is! At the end of the street! (*Shouts of "Hurrah!" etc., are heard.*) There's the leader! He's coming, he's coming nearer! (*Cries of acclaim and applause are heard from the wings.*) It's better if he doesn't see us... (*The* TWO ADMIRERS *hug the wall even closer.*) Watch out! (*The* ANNOUNCER *gives vent to a brief display of enthusiasm.*) Hurrah! Hurrah! The leader! The leader! Long live the leader! (*The* TWO ADMIRERS, *with their bodies rigid and flattened against the wall, thrust their necks and heads as far forward as they can to get a glimpse of the* LEADER.) The leader! The leader!

TWO ADMIRERS (*in unison*): Hurrah! Hurrah! (*Other "Hurrahs!" mingled with "Hurrah! Bravo!" come from the wings and gradually die down.*) Hurrah! Bravo!

(*The* ANNOUNCER *takes a step upstage, stops, then upstage, followed by the* TWO ADMIRERS, *saying as he goes: "Ah! Too bad! He's going away! He's going away! Follow me quickly! After him!" The* ANNOUNCER *and the* TWO ADMIRERS *leave, crying: "Leader! Leeeeader! Lee-ee-eader!" This last "Lee-ee-eader!" echoes in the wings like a bleating cry.*)

(*Silence. The stage is empty for a few brief moments. The* YOUNG LOVER *enters right, and his* GIRL FRIEND *left; they meet center stage.*)

YOUNG LOVER: Forgive me, Madame, or should I say Mademoiselle?

GIRL FRIEND: I beg your pardon, I'm afraid I don't happen to know you!

YOUNG LOVER: I beg your pardon, I'm afraid I don't know you either!

GIRL FRIEND: Then neither of us knows each other.

YOUNG LOVER: Exactly. We have something in common. It means that between us there is a basis of understanding on which we can build the edifice of our future.

GIRL FRIEND: That leaves me cold, I'm afraid. (*She makes as if to go.*)

YOUNG LOVER: Oh, my darling, I adore you.

GIRL FRIEND: Darling, so do I!
  (*They embrace.*)

YOUNG LOVER: I'm taking you with me, darling. We'll get married straightaway.
  (*They leave left. The stage is empty for a brief moment.*)

ANNOUNCER (*enters upstage followed by* TWO ADMIRERS): But the leader swore that he'd be passing here.

ADMIRER: Are you absolutely sure of that?

ANNOUNCER: Yes, yes, of course.

GIRL ADMIRER: Was it really on his way?

ANNOUNCER: Yes, yes. He should have passed by here, it was marked on the Festival program...

ADMIRER: Did you actually see it yourself and hear it with your own eyes and ears?

ANNOUNCER: He told someone. Someone else!

ADMIRER: But who? Who was this someone else?

GIRL ADMIRER: Was it a reliable person? A friend of yours?

ANNOUNCER: A friend of mine who I know very well. (*Suddenly in the background one hears renewed cries of "Hurrah!" and "Long live the leader!"*) That's him now! There he is! Hip! Hip! Hurrah! There he is! Hide yourselves! Hide yourselves!
  (*The* TWO ADMIRERS *flatten themselves as before against the wall, stretching their necks out toward the wings from where the shouts of acclamation come; the* ANNOUNCER *watches fixedly upstage, his back to the audience.*)

ANNOUNCER: The leader's coming. He approaches. He's bending. He's unbending. (*At each of the* ANNOUNCER's *words, the* ADMIRERS *give a start and stretch their necks even farther; they shudder.*) He's jumping. He's crossed the river. They're shaking his hand. He sticks out his thumb. Can you hear? They're laughing. (*The* ANNOUNCER *and the* TWO ADMIRERS *also laugh.*) Ah...! They're giving him a box of tools. What's he going to do with them? Ah...! He's signing autographs. The leader is stroking a hedgehog, a superb hedgehog! The crowd applauds. He's dancing, with the hedgehog in his hand. He's embracing his dancer. Hurrah! Hurrah! (*Cries are heard in the wings.*) He's being photographed, with his dancer on one hand and the hedgehog on the other....He greets the crowd....He spits a tremendous distance.

GIRL ADMIRER: Is he coming past here? Is he coming in our direction?

ADMIRER: Are we really on his route?

ANNOUNCER (*turns his head to the* TWO ADMIRERS): Quiet, and don't move, you're spoiling everything....

GIRL ADMIRER: But even so...

ANNOUNCER: Keep quiet, I tell you! Didn't I tell you he'd promised, that he fixed his itinerary himself....(*He turns back upstage and cries*): Hurrah! Hurrah! Long live the leader! (*Silence.*) Long live, long live the leader! (*Silence.*) Long live, long live, long live the leader-er!

TWO ADMIRERS (*unable to contain themselves, also give a sudden cry*): Hurrah! Long live the leader!

ANNOUNCER (*to the* ADMIRERS): Quiet, you two! Calm down! You're spoiling everything! (*Then, once more looking upstage, with the* ADMIRERS *silenced.*) Long live the leader! (*Wildly enthusiastic.*) Hurrah! Hurrah! He's

changing his shirt. He disappears behind a red
screen. He reappears! (*The applause intensifies.*)
Bravo! Bravo! (*The* ADMIRERS *also long to cry
"Bravo" and applaud; they put their hands to their
mouths to stop themselves.*) He's putting his tie
on! He's reading his newspaper and drinking his
morning coffee! He's still got his hedgehog...He's
leaning on the edge of the parapet. The parapet
breaks. He gets up...he gets up unaided! (*Applause, shouts of "Hurrah!"*) Bravo! Well done!
He brushes his soiled clothes.

TWO ADMIRERS (*stamping their feet*): Oh! Ah!
Oh! Oh! Ah! Ah!

ANNOUNCER: He's mounting the stool! He's
climbing piggyback, they're offering him a thin-
ended wedge, he knows it's meant as a joke, and he
doesn't mind, he's laughing.

(*Applause and enormous acclaim.*)

ADMIRER (*to the* GIRL ADMIRER): You hear
that? You hear? Oh! If I were king...

GIRL ADMIRER: Ah...! The leader! (*This is said
in an exalted tone.*)

ANNOUNCER (*still with his back to the public*):
He's mounting the stool. No. He's getting down. A
little girl offers him a bouquet of flowers...What's
he going to do? He takes the flowers....He
embraces the little girl....calls her "my child"...

ADMIRER: He embraces the little girl...calls her
"my child"...

GIRL ADMIRER: He embraces the little girl....calls
her "my child"...

ANNOUNCER: He gives her the hedgehog. The little girl's crying....Long live the leader! Long live
the lead-er!

ADMIRER: Is he coming past here?

GIRL ADMIRER: Is he coming past here?

ANNOUNCER (*with a sudden run, dashes out up-stage*): He's going away! Hurry! Come on! (*He disappears, followed by the TWO ADMIRERS, all crying "Hurrah! Hurrah!"*)

(*The stage is empty for a few moments. The TWO LOVERS enter, entwined in an embrace; they halt center stage and separate; she carries a basket on her arm.*)

GIRL FRIEND: Let's go to the market and get some eggs!

YOUNG LOVER: Oh! I love them as much as you do!

(*She takes his arm. From the right the AN-NOUNCER arrives running, quickly regaining his place, back to the public, followed closely by the TWO ADMIRERS, arriving one from the left and the other from the right; the TWO ADMIRERS knock into the TWO LOVERS who were about to leave right.*)

ADMIRER: Sorry!

YOUNG LOVER: Oh! Sorry!

GIRL ADMIRER: Sorry! Oh! Sorry!

GIRL FRIEND: Oh! Sorry, sorry, sorry, so sorry!

ADMIRER: Sorry, sorry, sorry, oh! sorry, sorry, so sorry!

YOUNG LOVER: Oh! oh, oh, oh, oh, oh! So sorry, everyone!

GIRL FRIEND (*to her LOVER*): Come along, Adolphe! (*To the TWO ADMIRERS.*) No harm done! (*She leaves, leading her LOVER by the hand.*)

ANNOUNCER (*watching upstage*): The leader is being pressed forward, and pressed back, and now they're pressing his trousers! (*The TWO ADMIRERS regain their places.*) The leader is smiling. Whilst they're pressing his trousers, he walks about. He tastes the flowers and the fruits growing in the stream. He's also tasting the roots of the trees. He suffers the little children to come unto him. He has confidence in everybody. He inaugurates the police force. He pays tribute to justice. He salutes the great victors and the great vanquished. Finally he recites a poem. The people are very moved.

TWO ADMIRERS: Bravo! Bravo! (*Then, sobbing.*) Boo! Boo! Boo!

ANNOUNCER: All the people are weeping. (*Loud cries are heard from the wings; the ANNOUNCER and the ADMIRERS also start to bellow.*) Silence! (*The TWO ADMIRERS fall silent; and there is silence from the wings.*) They've given the leader's trousers back. The leader puts them on. He looks happy! Hurrah! (*"Bravos," and acclaim from the wings. The TWO ADMIRERS also shout their acclaim, jump about, without being able to see anything of what is presumed to be happening in the wings.*) The leader's sucking his thumb! (*To the TWO ADMIRERS.*) Back, back, to your places, you two, don't move, behave yourselves and shout: "Long live the leader!"

TWO ADMIRERS (*flattened against the wall, shouting*): Long live, long live the leader!

ANNOUNCER: Be quiet, I tell you, you'll spoil everything! Look out, the leader's coming!

ANNOUNCER: (*in the same position*): The leader's coming!

GIRL ADMIRER: The leader's coming!

ANNOUNCER: Watch out! And keep quiet! Oh! The leader's going away! Follow him! Follow me!

(*The ANNOUNCER goes out upstage, running; the TWO ADMIRERS leave right and left, whilst in the wings the acclaim mounts, then fades. The stage is momentarily empty. The* YOUNG LOVER, *followed by his* GIRL FRIEND, *appears left running across the stage right.)*

YOUNG LOVER (*running*): You won't catch me! You won't catch me! (*Goes out.*)

GIRL FRIEND (*running*): Wait a moment! Wait a moment! (*She goes out.*)

(*The stage is empty for a moment; then once more the* TWO LOVERS *cross the stage at a run, and leave.*)

YOUNG LOVER: You won't catch me!

GIRL FRIEND: Wait a moment!

(*They leave right. The stage is empty. The AN-NOUNCER reappears upstage, the ADMIRER from the right, the GIRL ADMIRER from the left. They meet center.*)

ADMIRER: We missed him!

GIRL ADMIRER: Rotten luck!

ANNOUNCER: It was your fault!

ADMIRER: That's not true!

GIRL ADMIRER: No, that's not true!

ANNOUNCER: Are you suggesting it was mine?

ADMIRER: No, we didn't mean that!

GIRL ADMIRER: No, we didn't mean that!

(*Noise of acclaim and "Hurrahs" from the wings.*)

ANNOUNCER: Hurrah!

GIRL ADMIRER: It's from over there! (*She points upstage.*)

ADMIRER: Yes, it's from over there! (*He points left.*)

ANNOUNCER: Very well. Follow me! Long live the leader! (*He runs out right, followed by the* TWO ADMIRERS, *also shouting.*)

TWO ADMIRERS: Long live the leader! (*They leave.*)

> (*The stage is empty for a moment. The* YOUNG LOVER *and his* GIRL FRIEND *appear left; the* YOUNG LOVER *exits upstage; the* GIRL FRIEND *after saying "I'll get you!" runs out right. The* ANNOUNCER *and the* TWO ADMIRERS *appear from upstage.*)

ANNOUNCER: (*to the* ADMIRERS): Long live the leader! (*This is repeated by the* ADMIRERS. *Then, still talking to the* ADMIRERS.) Follow me! Follow the leader! (*He leaves upstage, still running and shouting.*) Follow him!

> (*The* ADMIRER *exits right, the* GIRL ADMIRER *left into the wings. During the whole of this, the acclaim is heard louder or fainter according to the rhythm of the stage action; the stage is empty for a moment, then the* LOVERS *appear from right and left, crying:*)

YOUNG LOVER: I'll get you!

GIRL FRIEND: You won't get me!

> (*They leave at a run, shouting: "Long live the leader!" the* ANNOUNCER *and the* TWO ADMIRERS *emerge from upstage, also shouting: "Long live the leader," followed by the* TWO LOVERS. *They all leave right, in single file, crying as they run: "The leader! Long live the leader! We'll get him! It's from over here! You won't get me!"*)

> (*They enter and leave, employing all the exits; finally, entering from left, from right, and from upstage they all meet center, whilst the acclaim and the applause from the wings become a fearful din. They embrace each other feverishly, crying at the tops of their voices: "Long live the leader! Long live the leader! Long live the lead-*

er!" *Then, abruptly, silence falls.*)

ANNOUNCER: The leader is arriving. Here's the leader. To your places! Attention!

(*The ADMIRER and the GIRL FRIEND flatten themselves against the wall right; the GIRL ADMIRER and the YOUNG LOVER against the wall left; the two couples are in each other's arms, embracing.*)

ADMIRER *and* GIRL FRIEND: My dear, my darling!

GIRL ADMIRER *and* YOUNG LOVER: My dear, my darling!

(*Meanwhile the ANNOUNCER has taken up his place, back to the audience, looking fixedly upstage; a lull in the applause.*)

ANNOUNCER: Silence. The leader has eaten his soup. He is coming. He is nigh.

(*The acclaim redoubles its intensity; the TWO ADMIRERS and the TWO LOVERS shout.*)

ALL: Hurrah! Hurrah! Long live the leader!

(*They throw confetti before he arrives. Then the ANNOUNCER hurls himself suddenly to one side to allow the LEADER to pass; the other four characters freeze with outstretched arms holding confetti; but still say: "Hurrah!" The LEADER enters from upstage, advances downstage to center; to the footlights, hesitates, takes a step to left, then makes a decision, and leaves with great, energetic strides by right, to the enthusiastic "Hurrahs!" of the ANNOUNCER and the feeble, somewhat astonished "Hurrahs!" of the other four; these, in fact, have some reason to be surprised, as the LEADER is headless, though wearing a hat. This is simple to effect: the actor playing the LEADER needing only to wear an overcoat with the collar turned* up round his forehead and topped with a hat. *The-man-in-an-overcoat-with-a-hat-with-out-a-head* is a somewhat surprising apparition and will doubtless produce a certain sensation.)

GIRL ADMIRER (*after the* LEADER's *disappearance*): But...but...the leader hasn't got a head!

ANNOUNCER: What's he need a head for when he's got genius!

YOUNG LOVER: That's true! (*To the* GIRL FRIEND.) What's your name!

(*The* YOUNG LOVER *to the* GIRL ADMIRER, *the* GIRL ADMIRER *to the* ANNOUNCER, *the* ANNOUNCER *to the* GIRL FRIEND, *the* GIRL FRIEND *to the* YOUNG LOVER): What's yours? What's yours? What's yours? (*Then, all together, one to the other.*) What's your name?

CURTAIN

Status Symbol

i
Have arrived

i
am the
New Negro

i
am the result of
President Lincoln
World War I
and Paris
the
Red Ball Express
white drinking fountains
sitdowns and
sit-ins
Federal troops
Marches on Washington
and
prayer meetings...

today
They hired me
it
is a status
job...
along
with my papers
They
gave me my
Status Symbol
the
key
to the
White...Locked...
John

Mari E. Evans

The Politician

Behold the politician.
Self-preservation is his ambition.
He thrives in the D. of C.,
Where he was sent by you and me.

Whether elected or appointed
He considers himself the Lord's anointed,
And indeed the ointment lingers on him
So thick you can't get your fingers on him.

He has developed a sixth sense
About living at the public expense,
Because in private competition
He would encounter malnutrition.

He has many profitable hobbies
Not the least of which is lobbies.
He would not sell his grandmother for a quarter
If he suspected the presence of a reporter.

He gains votes ever and anew
By taking money from everybody and giving it to a
    few,
While explaining that every penny
Was extracted from the few to be given to the many.

Some politicians are Republican, some Democratic,
And their feud is dramatic,
But except for the name
They are identically the same.

Ogden Nash

a spider
and a fly

i heard a spider
and a fly arguing
wait said the fly
do not eat me
i serve a great purpose
in the world

you will have to
show me said the spider

i scurry around
gutters and sewers
and garbage cans
said the fly and gather
up the germs of
typhoid influenza
and pneumonia on my feet

and wings
then i carry these germs
into the households of men
and give them diseases
all the people who
have lived the right
sort of life recover
from the diseases
and the old soaks who
have weakened their systems
with liquor and iniquity
succumb it is my mission
to help rid the world
of these wicked persons
i am a vessel of righteousness
scattering seeds of justice
and serving the noblest uses

it is true said the spider
that you are more
useful in a plodding
material sort of way
than i am but i do not
serve the utilitarian deities
i serve the gods of beauty
look at the gossamer webs
i weave they float in the sun
like filaments of song
if you get what i mean
i do not work at anything
i play all the time
i am busy with the stuff
of enchantment and the materials
of fairyland my works

transcend utility
i am the artist
a creator and a demigod
it is ridiculous to suppose
that i should be denied
the food i need in order
to continue to create
beauty i tell you
plainly mister fly it is all
damned nonsense for that food
to rear up on its hind legs
and say it should not be eaten

you have convinced me
said the fly say no more
and shutting all his eyes
he prepared himself for dinner
and yet he said i could
have made out a case
for myself too if i had
had a better line of talk

of course you could said the spider
clutching a sirloin from him
but the end would have been
just the same if neither of
us had spoken at all

boss i am afraid that what
the spider said is true
and it gives me to think
furiously upon the futility
of literature

                    archy

        Don Marquis

Thomas Gradgrind

by Charles Dickens

"Now, what I want is, Facts. Teach these boys and girls nothing but Facts. Facts alone are wanted in life. Plant nothing else, and root out everything else. You can only form the minds of reasoning animals upon Facts; nothing else will ever be of any service to them. This is the principle on which I bring up my own children, and this is the principle on which I bring up these children. Stick to Facts, sir!"

The scene was a plain, bare, monotonous vault of a schoolroom, and the speaker's square forefinger emphasized his observations by underscoring every sentence with a line on the schoolmaster's sleeve. The emphasis was helped by the speaker's square wall of a forehead, which had his eyebrows for its base, while his eyes found commodious cellarage in two dark caves, overshadowed by the wall. The emphasis was helped by the speaker's mouth, which was wide, thin, and hard set. The emphasis was helped by the speaker's voice, which was inflexible, dry, and dictatorial. The emphasis was helped by the speaker's hair, which bristled on the skirts of his bald head, a plantation of firs to keep the wind from its shining surface, all covered with knobs, like the crust of a plum pie, as if the head had scarcely warehouse-room for the hard facts stored inside. The speaker's obstinate carriage, square coat, square legs, square shoulders — nay, his very neckcloth, trained to take him by the throat with an unaccommodating grasp, like a stubborn fact, as it was — all helped the emphasis.

"In this life, we want nothing but Facts, sir; nothing but Facts!"

The speaker, and the schoolmaster, and the third grown person present, all backed a little, and swept with their eyes the inclined plane of little vessels then and there arranged in order, ready to have imperial gallons of facts poured into them until they were full to the brim.

THOMAS GRADGRIND, sir. A man of realities. A man of facts and calculations. A man who proceeds upon the principle that two and two are four, and nothing over, and who is not to be talked into allowing for anything over. Thomas Gradgrind, sir — peremptorily Thomas — Thomas Gradgrind. With a rule and a pair of scales, and the multiplication table always in his pocket, sir, ready to weigh and measure any parcel of human nature, and tell you exactly what it comes to. It is a mere question of figures, a case of simple arithmetic. You might hope to get some other nonsensical belief into the head of George Gradgrind, or Augustus Gradgrind, or John Gradgrind, or Joseph Gradgrind (all nonexistent persons), but into the head of Thomas Gradgrind — no, sir!

In such terms Mr. Gradgrind always mentally introduced himself, whether to his private circle of acquaintance, or to the public in general. In such terms, no doubt, substituting the words "boys and girls" for "sir," Thomas Gradgrind now presented Thomas Gradgrind to the little pitchers before him, who were to be filled so full of facts.

Indeed, as he eagerly sparkled at them from the cellarage before mentioned, he seemed a kind of cannon loaded to the muzzle with facts, and prepared to blow them clean out of the regions of childhood at one discharge. He seemed a galvanizing apparatus too, charged with a grim mechanical substitute for the tender young imaginations that were to be stormed away.

"Girl number 20," said Mr. Gradgrind, squarely pointing with his square forefinger, "I don't know that girl. Who is that girl?"

"Sissy Jupe, sir," explained number 20, standing up, and curtseying.

"Sissy is not a name," said Mr. Gradgrind. "Don't call yourself Sissy. Call yourself Cecilia."

"It's father as calls me Sissy, sir," returned the young girl in a trembling voice, and with another curtsey.

"Then he has no business to do it," said Mr. Gradgrind. "Tell him he mustn't. Cecilia Jupe. Let me see. What is your father?"

"He belongs to the horse-riding, if you please, sir."

Mr. Gradgrind frowned, and waved off the objectionable calling with his hand.

"We don't want to know anything about that, here. You mustn't tell us about that, here. Your father breaks horses, don't he?"

"If you please, sir, when they can get any to break,

they do break horses in the ring, sir."

"You mustn't tell us about the ring here. Very well, then. Describe your father as a horsebreaker. He doctors sick horses, I daresay?"

"Oh, yes, sir."

"Very well, then. He is a veterinary surgeon, a farrier, and horsebreaker. Give me your definition of a horse."

(Sissy Jupe is thrown into the greatest alarm by this demand.)

"Girl number 20 unable to define a horse!" said Mr. Gradgrind, for the general behoof of all the little pitchers. "Girl number 20 possessed of no facts in reference to one of the commonest of animals! Some boy's definition of a horse. Bitzer, yours."

The square finger, moving here and there, lighted suddenly on Bitzer, perhaps because he chanced to sit in the same ray of sunlight which, darting in at one of the bare windows of the intensely whitewashed room, irradiated Sissy. For, the boys and girls sat on the face of the inclined plane in two compact bodies, divided up the center by a narrow interval; and Sissy, being at the corner of a row on the sunny side, came in for the beginning of a sunbeam, of which Bitzer, being at the corner of a row on the other side, a few rows in advance, caught the end. But, whereas the girl was so dark-eyed and dark-haired that she seemed to receive a deeper and more lustrous color from the sun, when it shone upon her, the boy was so light-eyed and light-haired that the self-same rays appeared to draw out of him what little color he ever possessed. His cold eyes would hardly have been eyes, but for the short ends of lashes which, by bringing them into immediate contrast with something paler than themselves, expressed their form. His short-cropped hair might have been a mere continuation of the sandy freckles on his forehead and face. His skin was so unwholesomely deficient in the natural tinge, that he looked as though, if cut, he would bleed white.

"Bitzer," said Thomas Gradgrind. "Your definition of a horse."

"Quadruped. Graminivorous. Forty teeth, namely 24 grinders, four eyeteeth, and 12 incisive. Sheds coat in the spring; in marshy countries, sheds hoofs too. Hoofs hard, but requiring to be shod with iron. Age known by marks in mouth." Thus (and much more) Bitzer.

"Now, girl number 20," said Mr. Gradgrind, "you know what a horse is."

She curtseyed again, and would have blushed deeper, if she could have blushed deeper than she had blushed all this time. Bitzer, after rapidly blinking at Thomas Gradgrind with both eyes at once, and so catching the light upon his quivering ends of lashes that they looked like the antennae of busy insects, put his knuckles to his freckled forehead, and sat down again.

The third gentleman now stepped forth. A mighty man at cutting and drying, he was; a government officer; in his way (and in most other people's too), a professed pugilist; always in training, always with a system to force down the general throat like a bolus, always to be heard of at the bar of his little public office, ready to fight all England. To continue in the fistic phraseology, he had a genius for coming up to the scratch, wherever and whatever it was, and proving himself an ugly customer. He would go in and damage any subject whatever with his right, follow up with his left, stop, exchange, counter, bore his opponent (he always fought All England) to the ropes, and fall upon him neatly. He was certain to knock the wind out of common sense, and render that unlucky adversary deaf to the call of time. And he had it in charge from high authority to bring about the great public-office millennium, when commissioners should reign upon earth.

"Very well," said this gentleman, briskly smiling, and folding his arms. "That's a horse. Now, let me ask you, girls and boys, Would you paper a room with representations of horses?"

After a pause, one half of the children cried in chorus, "Yes, sir!" Upon which the other half, seeing in the gentleman's face that Yes was wrong, cried out in chorus, "No, sir" — as the custom is, in these examinations.

"Of course, No. Why wouldn't you?"

A pause. One corpulent slow boy, with a wheezy manner of breathing, ventured the answer, Because he wouldn't paper a room at all, but would paint it.

"You *must* paper it," said the gentleman, rather warmly.

"You must paper it," said Thomas Gradgrind, "whether you like it or not. Don't tell *us* you wouldn't paper it. What do you mean, boy?"

"I'll explain to you, then," said the gentleman, after another and a dismal pause, "why you wouldn't paper a room with representations of horses. Do you ever see horses walking up and down the sides of rooms in reality — in fact? Do you?"

"Yes, sir!" from one half. "No, sir!" from the other.

"Of course, No," said the gentleman, with an indignant look at the wrong half. "Why, then, you are not to see anywhere what you don't see in fact; you are not to have anywhere what you don't have in fact. What is called Taste, is only another name for Fact."

Thomas Gradgrind nodded his approbation.

"This is a new principle, a discovery, a great discovery," said the gentleman. "Now I'll try you again. Suppose you were going to carpet a room. Would you use a carpet having a representation of flowers upon it?"

There being a general conviction by this time that "No, sir!" was always the right answer to this gentleman, the chorus of No was very strong. Only a few feeble stragglers said Yes; among them Sissy Jupe.

"Girl number 20," said the gentleman, smiling in the calm strength of knowledge.

Sissy blushed, and stood up.

"So you would carpet your room — or your husband's room, if you were a grown woman, and had a husband — with representations of flowers, would you," said the gentleman. "Why would you?"

"If you please, sir, I am very fond of flowers," returned the girl.

"And is that why you would put tables and chairs upon them, and have people walking over them with heavy boots?"

"It wouldn't hurt them, sir. They wouldn't crush and wither if you please, sir. They would be the pictures of what was very pretty and pleasant, and I would fancy — "

"Ay, ay, ay! But you mustn't fancy," cried the gentleman, quite elated by coming so happily to his point. "That's it! You are never to fancy."

"You are not, Cecilia Jupe," Thomas Gradgrind solemnly repeated, "to do anything of that kind."

"Fact, fact, fact!" said the gentleman. And "Fact, fact, fact!" repeated Thomas Gradgrind.

"You are to be in all things regulated and governed," said the gentleman, "by fact. We hope to have before long, a board of fact, composed of commissioners of fact, who will force the people to be a people of fact, and of nothing but fact. You must discard the word "fancy" altogether. You have nothing to do with it. You are not to have, in any object of use or ornament, what would be a contradiction in fact. You don't walk upon flowers in fact; you cannot be allowed to walk upon flowers in carpets. You don't find that foreign birds and butterflies come and perch upon your crockery; you cannot be permitted to paint foreign birds and butterflies upon your crockery. You never meet quadrupeds going up and down walls; you must not have quadrupeds represented upon walls. You must use," said the gentleman, "for all these purposes, combinations and modifications (in primary colors) of mathematical figures which are susceptible of proof and demonstration. This is the new discovery! This is Fact. This is taste."

© 1961 Saul Steinberg. From *The New World* (Harper & Row). Originally in The New Yorker.

Illustration by John Tenniel

Humpty Dumpty

by Lewis Carroll

Humpty Dumpty was sitting, with his legs crossed like a Turk, on the top of a high wall — such a narrow one that Alice quite wondered how he could keep his balance — and, as his eyes were steadily fixed in the opposite direction, and he didn't take the least notice of her, she thought he must be a stuffed figure, after all.

"And how exactly like an egg he is!" she said aloud, standing with her hands ready to catch him, for she was every moment expecting him to fall.

"It's *very* provoking," Humpty Dumpty said after a long silence, looking away from Alice as he spoke, "to be called an egg — *very!*"

"I said you *looked* like an egg, sir," Alice gently explained. "And some eggs are very pretty, you know," she added, hoping to turn her remark into a sort of compliment.

"Some people," said Humpty Dumpty, looking

away from her as usual, "have no more sense than a baby!"

Alice didn't know what to say to this. It wasn't at all like conversation, she thought, as he never said anything to *her*; in fact, his last remark was evidently addressed to a tree — so she stood and softly repeated to herself:

> *"Humpty Dumpty sat on a wall:*
> *Humpty Dumpty had a great fall.*
> *All the King's horses and all the King's men*
> *Couldn't put Humpty Dumpty in his place*
>   *again."*

"That last line is much too long for the poetry," she added, almost out loud, forgetting that Humpty Dumpty would hear her.

"Don't stand chattering to yourself like that," Humpty Dumpty said, looking at her for the first time, "but tell me your name and your business."

"My *name* is Alice, but — "

"It's a stupid name enough!" Humpty Dumpty interrupted impatiently. "What does it mean?"

"*Must* a name mean something?" Alice asked doubtfully.

"Of course it must," Humpty Dumpty said with a short laugh: "*my* name means the shape I am — and a good handsome shape it is too. With a name like yours, you might be any shape, almost."

"Why do you sit out here all alone?" said Alice, not wishing to begin an argument.

"Why, because there's nobody with me!" cried Humpty Dumpty. "Did you think I didn't know the answer to *that*? Ask another."

"Don't you think you'd be safer down on the ground?" Alice went on, not with any idea of making another riddle, but simply in her good-natured anxiety for the queer creature. "That wall is so *very* narrow!"

"What tremendously easy riddles you ask!" Humpty Dumpty growled out. "Of course I don't think so! Why, if ever I *did* fall off — which there's no chance of — but *if* I did — " Here he pursed up his lips, and looked so solemn and grand that Alice could hardly help laughing. "*If I did* fall," he went on, "*the King has promised me* — ah, you may turn pale, if you like! You didn't think I was going to say that, did you? *The King has promised me — with his very own mouth* — to — to — "

"To send all his horses and all his men," Alice interrupted, rather unwisely.

"Now I declare that's too bad!" Humpty Dumpty cried, breaking into a sudden passion. "You've been listening at doors — and behind trees — and down chimneys — or you couldn't have known it!"

"I haven't, indeed!" Alice said very gently. "It's in a book."

"Ah, well! They may write such things in a *book*," Humpty Dumpty said in a calmer tone. "That's what you call a History of England, that is. Now, take a good look at me! I'm one that has spoken to a King, *I* am: mayhap you'll never see such another: and, to show you I'm not proud, you may shake hands with me!" And he grinned almost from ear to ear, as he leaned forward (and as nearly as possible fell off the wall in doing so) and offered Alice his hand. She watched him a little anxiously as she took it. "If he smiled much more the ends of his mouth might meet behind," she thought: "and then I don't know what would happen to his head! I'm afraid it would come off!"

"Yes, all his horses and all his men," Humpty

Dumpty went on. "They'd pick me up again in a minute, *they* would! However, this conversation is going on a little too fast: Let's go back to the last remark but one."

"I'm afraid I can't quite remember it," Alice said, very politely.

"In that case we start afresh," said Humpty Dumpty, "and it's my turn to choose a subject —" ("He talks about it just as if it was a game!" thought Alice.) "So here's a question for you. How old did you say you were?"

Alice made a short calculation, and said, "Seven years and six months."

"Wrong!" Humpty Dumpty exclaimed triumphantly. "You never said a word like it!"

"I thought you meant 'How old *are* you?'" Alice explained.

"If I'd meant that, I'd have said it," said Humpty Dumpty.

Alice didn't want to begin another argument, so she said nothing.

"Seven years and six months!" Humpty Dumpty repeated thoughtfully. "An uncomfortable sort of age. Now if you'd asked *my* advice, I'd have said, 'Leave off at seven' — but it's too late now."

"I never ask advice about growing," Alice said indignantly.

"Too proud?" the other enquired.

Alice felt even more indignant at this suggestion. "I mean," she said, "that one can't help growing older."

"*One* can't, perhaps," said Humpty Dumpty; "but *two* can. With proper assistance, you might have left off at seven."

"What a beautiful belt you've got on!" Alice suddenly remarked. (They had had quite enough of the subject of age, she thought: and, if they really were to take turns in choosing subjects, it was *her* turn now.) "At least," she corrected herself on second thought, "a beautiful cravat, I should have said — no, a belt, I mean — I beg your pardon!" she added in dismay, for Humpty Dumpty looked thoroughly offended, and she began to wish she hadn't chosen that subject. "If only I knew," she thought to herself, "which was neck and which was waist!"

Evidently Humpty Dumpty was very angry, though he said nothing for a minute or two. When he *did* speak again, it was in a deep growl.

"It is a — *most — provoking* — thing," he said at last, "when a person doesn't know a cravat from a belt!"

"I know it's very ignorant of me," Alice said, in so humble a tone that Humpty Dumpty relented.

"It's a cravat, child, and a beautiful one, as you say. It's a present from the White King and Queen. There now!"

"Is it really?" said Alice, quite pleased to find that she *had* chosen a good subject, after all.

"They gave it me," Humpty continued thoughtfully, as he crossed one knee over the other and clasped his hands round it, "they gave it me — for an un-birthday present."

"I beg your pardon?" Alice said with a puzzled air.

"I'm not offended," said Humpty Dumpty.

"I mean, what *is* an un-birthday present?"

"A present given when it isn't your birthday, of course."

Alice considered a little. "I like birthday presents best," she said at last.

"You don't know what you're talking about!" cried Humpty Dumpty. "How many days are there in a year?"

"Three hundred and sixty-five," said Alice.

"And how many birthdays have you?"

"One."

"And if you take one from 365, what remains?"

"Three hundred and sixty-four, of course."

Humpty Dumpty looked doubtful. "I'd rather see that done on paper," he said.

Alice couldn't help smiling as she took out her memorandum book, and worked the sum for him:

$$
\begin{array}{r}
365 \\
1 \\
\hline
364
\end{array}
$$

Humpty Dumpty took the book, and looked at it carefully. "That seems to be done right — " he began.

"You're holding it upside down!" Alice interrupted.

"To be sure I was!" Humpty Dumpty said gaily, as she turned it round for him. "I thought it looked a little queer. As I was saying, that *seems* to be done right — though I haven't time to look it over thoroughly just now — and that shows that there are 364 days when you might get un-birthday presents — "

"Certainly," said Alice.

"And only *one* for birthday presents, you know. There's glory for you!" he said.

"I don't know what you mean by 'glory.'"

Humpty Dumpty smiled contemptuously. "Of course you don't — till I tell you. I meant 'there's a nice knockdown argument for you!'"

"But 'glory' doesn't mean a 'nice knockdown argument,'" Alice objected.

"When *I* use a word," Humpty Dumpty said, in rather a scornful tone, "it means just what I choose it to mean — neither more nor less."

"The question is," said Alice, "whether you *can* make words mean so many different things."

"The question is," said Humpty Dumpty, "which is to be master — that's all."

Alice was too much puzzled to say anything; so after a minute Humpty Dumpty began again. "They've a temper, some of them — particularly verbs: they're the proudest — adjectives you can do anything with, but not verbs — however, *I* can manage the whole lot of them! Impenetrability! That's what *I* say!"

"Would you tell me, please," said Alice, "what that means?"

"Now you talk like a reasonable child," said Humpty Dumpty, looking very much pleased. "I meant by 'impenetrability' that we've had enough of that subject, and it would be just as well if you'd mention what you mean to do next, as I suppose you don't mean to stop here all the rest of your life."

"That's a great deal to make one word mean," Alice said in a thoughtful tone.

"When I make a word do a lot of work like that," said Humpty Dumpty, "I always pay it extra."

"Oh!" said Alice. She was too much puzzled to make any other remark.

"Ah, you should see 'em come round me of a Saturday night," Humpty Dumpty went on, wagging his head gravely from side to side, "for to get their wages, you know."

(Alice didn't venture to ask what he paid them with; and so you see I can't tell *you*.)

"You seem very clever at explaining words, sir," said Alice. "Would you kindly tell me the meaning of the poem called 'Jabberwocky'?"

"Let's hear it," said Humpty Dumpty. "I can explain all the poems that ever were invented — and a good many that haven't been invented just yet."

This sounded very hopeful, so Alice repeated the first verse:

> " 'Twas brillig, and the slithy toves
> Did gyre and gimble in the wabe:
> All mimsy were the borogoves,
> And the mome raths outgrabe."

"That's enough to begin with," Humpty Dumpty interrupted: "there are plenty of hard words there. 'Brillig' means four o'clock in the afternoon — the time when you begin *broiling* things for dinner."

"That'll do very well," said Alice: "and 'slithy'?"

"Well, 'slithy' means 'lithe and slimy.' 'Lithe' is the same as 'active.' You see it's like a portmanteau — there are two meanings packed up into one word."

"I see it now," Alice remarked thoughtfully: "and what are 'toves'?"

"Well, 'toves' are something like badgers — they're something like lizards — and they're something like corkscrews."

"They must be very curious-looking creatures."

"They are that," said Humpty Dumpty: "also they make their nests under sundials — also they live on cheese."

"And what's to 'gyre' and to 'gimble'?"

"To 'gyre' is to go round and round like a gyroscope. To 'gimble' is to make holes like a gimblet."

"And 'the wabe' is the grass plot round a sundial, I suppose?" said Alice, surprised at her own ingenuity.

"Of course it is. It's called 'wabe,' you know, because it goes a long way before it, and a long way behind it — "

"And a long way beyond it on each side," Alice added.

"Exactly so. Well then, 'mimsy' is 'flimsy and miserable' (there's another portmanteau for you). And a 'borogove' is a thin shabby-looking bird with its feathers sticking out all round — something like a live mop."

"And then 'mome raths'?" said Alice. "I'm afraid I'm giving you a great deal of trouble."

"Well, a 'rath' is a sort of green pig: But 'mome' I'm not certain about. I think it's short for 'from home' — meaning that they'd lost their way, you know."

"And what does 'outgrabe' mean?"

"Well, 'outgribing' is something between bellowing and whistling, with a kind of sneeze in the middle: However, you'll hear it done, maybe — down in the wood yonder — and, when you've once heard it, you'll be quite content. Who's been repeating all that hard stuff to you?"

"I read it in a book," said Alice.

WORLD'S HIGHEST

Photograph by Margaret Bourke-White   TIME-LIFE Picture Agency

Motive

STANDARD OF LIVING

There's no way like the American Way

The Latest Decalogue

Thou shalt have one God only; who
Would be at the expense of two?
No graven images may be
Worshiped, except the currency.
Swear not at all; for, for thy curse
Thine enemy is none the worse.
At church on Sunday to attend
Will serve to keep the world thy friend.
Honour thy parents; that is, all
From whom advancement may befall.
Thou shalt not kill; but need'st not strive
Officiously to keep alive.
Do not adultery commit;
Advantage rarely comes of it.
Thou shalt not steal; an empty feat,
When it's so lucrative to cheat.
Bear not false witness, let the lie
Have time on its own wings to fly.
Thou shalt not covet, but tradition
Approves all forms of competition.

Arthur Hugh Clough

Hod Putt

Here I lie close to the grave
Of Old Bill Piersol,
Who grew rich trading with the Indians, and who
Afterward took the bankrupt law
And emerged from it richer than ever.
Myself grown tired of toil and poverty
And beholding how Old Bill and others grew in
  wealth,
Robbed a traveler one night near Proctor's Grove,
Killing him unwittingly while doing so,
For the which I was tried and hanged.
That was my way of going into bankruptcy.
Now we who took the bankrupt law in our respective
  ways
Sleep peacefully side by side.

Edgar Lee Masters

Miss Kindergarten America

by Carol Schacter

Miss Kindergarten America of 1984 hitched up her garters and teetered back to her hotel room overlooking the boardwalk. She was a very small beauty queen and it had been a tiring day, the most exciting day of her whole life. She had done it! She had won the title and next year, Mommy promised, she could enter the preliminaries for the Miss Pre-Sub-Teen America pageant. Oh, Mommy was so happy!

As soon as she closed her door, she stepped out of her high heels and ripped off her girdle. Gee, that felt good! Standing all afternoon at the Coketail press party had been awful.

She undressed and stood at the mirror, looking at her figure. When she had reached the semifinals, she had stopped eating cookies and ice cream and started smoking. Then she had really lost a lot of weight. Daddy called it "baby fat" and said leave it alone, but Mommy said after all, the child *is* five and it's about time she thought about her shape. (She didn't really like the taste of cigarettes too much, but ever since the sixth graders got their own smoking lounge at school, all the younger kids sneaked a few drags at recess, hiding under the slide. And then it got to be a habit.)

She carefully removed her makeup with Big Idea Moisturizing Cleanser, slapped on some Big Idea Skin Freshener and Big Idea Hormone Night Cream. She considered not setting her hair but knew it was hopeless. Her perm was growing out and this morning Kenneth had teased her hair so much (to make it look natural), she knew it would collapse overnight. Maybe she'd run in for a comb-out after breakfast.

A half hour later all the rollers were in place and she rubbed her aching arms. She laid out her dress for the next day's festivities — a stunning little nothing from Saks, all shape and line. She'd be able to wear it to the PTA first-grade dancing classes next year, so $89.95 wasn't really expensive. Even Mommy had said it was a thoughtful investment.

She set her clock-TV for 6:30 and tucked in her doll family for the night. Santa Claus had brought her the whole set last Christmas. It came in a big box with three double beds and a new educational toy, "The Mating Game." There was Grandma Barbie and Grandpa Ken and Daughter Sally and Son-in-Law Rob and their daughter Lolly and her boyfriend Tom. Sally came equipped with snap-on bosoms and snap-on tummies and a yummy wardrobe of maternity clothes so you could pretend she was in all different "months."

She got under the covers and lay on her side, her arms and legs curled up under her chin. The rollers hurt like anything. She thought how nice it would be to go home and see Daddy. She really hadn't spent much time with him since Tabitha Carleton's fifth-birthday coming-out party. Ever since that night, she'd been busy working for the title.

The party had been lots of fun but, gee, what a mess after those third-grade boys crashed it and spiked all the the Cokes. All those broken windows and doll furniture thrown all over the beach....But still, it was the publicity that had started her on the road to the crown. Mommy took her straight to the modeling agency in New York, and she hadn't been so busy since she was three and a cheerleader for the Little Punks Tiny Football League. Now here she was, at last, Miss Kindergarten America.

She tried and tried to find a comfortable position but something didn't feel quite right. Something was missing. Then she remembered and ran over to the closet. Oh good! No one had found the bag she had stuffed behind her mink stole. She went back to bed. With her mangy teddy bear, an old plush elephant, and a somewhat soiled rag doll cuddled fiercely in her arms, she fell sound asleep.

The Selling
of Tono-Bungay

by H. G. Wells

So I made my peace with my uncle, and we set out upon this bright enterprise of selling slightly injurious rubbish at one-and-three-halfpence and two-and-nine a bottle, including the government stamp. We made Tono-Bungay hum! It brought us wealth, influence, respect, the confidence of endless people. All that my uncle promised me proved truth and understatement; Tono-Bungay carried me to freedoms and powers that no life of scientific research, no passionate service of humanity could ever have given me....

It was my uncle's genius that did it. No doubt he needed me — I was, I will admit, his indispensable right hand; but his was the brain to conceive. He wrote every advertisement; some of them even he sketched. You must remember that his were the days before the *Times* took to enterprise and the vociferous hawking of that antiquated *Encyclopaedia*. That alluring, buttonholing, let-me-just-tell-you-quite-soberly-something-you-ought-to-know style of newspaper advertisement, with every now and then a convulsive jump of some attractive phrase into capitals, was then almost a novelty. "Many people who are MODERATELY well think they are QUITE well," was one of his early efforts. The jerks in capitals were, "DO NOT NEED DRUGS OR MEDICINE," and "SIMPLY A PROPER REGIMEN TO GET YOU IN TONE." One was warned against the chemist or druggist who pushed "much-advertised nostrums" on one's attention. That trash did more harm than good. The thing needed was regimen — and Tono-Bungay!

Very early too was that bright little quarter column, at least it was usually a quarter column in the evening papers: "HILARITY — TONO-BUNGAY. Like Mountain Air in the Veins." The penetrating trio of questions: "Are you bored with your Business? Are you bored with your Dinner? Are you bored with your Wife?" — that too was in our Gower Street days. Both these we had in our first campaign when we worked London south, central, and west; and then too we had our first poster — the HEALTH, BEAUTY, AND STRENGTH one. That was his design; I happen still to have got by me the first sketch he made for it.

These things were only incidental in my department. I had to polish them up for the artist and arrange the business of printing and distribution, and after my uncle had had a violent and needless quarrel with the advertising manager of the *Daily Regulator* about the amount of display given to one of his happy thoughts, I also took up the negotiations of advertisements for the press.

We discussed and worked out distribution together — first on the drawing-room floor in Gower Street with my aunt sometimes helping very shrewdly, and then, with a steadily improving type of cigar and older and older whiskey, in his snuggery at their first house, the one in Beckenham. Often we worked far into the night — sometimes until dawn.

We really worked infernally hard, and, I recall, we worked with very decided enthusiam, not simply on my uncle's part but mine. It was a game, an absurd but absurdly interesting game, and the points were scored in cases of bottles. People think a happy notion is enough to make a man rich, that fortunes can be made without toil. It's a dream, as every millionaire (except one or two lucky gamblers) can testify; I doubt if J. D. Rockefeller in the early days of Standard Oil worked harder than we did. We worked far into the night — and we also worked all day. We made a rule to be always dropping in at the factory unannounced to keep things right — for at first we could afford no properly responsible underlings — and we traveled to London, pretending to be our own representatives and making all sorts of special arrangements.

But none of this was my special work, and as soon as we could get other men in, I dropped the traveling, though my uncle found it particularly interesting and kept it up for years. "Does me good, George, to see the chaps behind their counters like I was once," he explained. My special and distinctive duty was to give Tono-Bungay substance and an outward and visible bottle, to translate my uncle's great imaginings into the creation of case after case of labeled bottles of nonsense, and the punctual discharge of them by railway, road, and steamer toward the ultimate goal in the Great Stomach of the People. By all modern standards the business was, as my uncle would say, "absolutely bona fide." We sold our stuff and got the money, and spent the money honestly in lies and clamor to sell more stuff. Section by section we spread it over the whole of the British Isles; first working the middle-class London suburbs, then the outer suburbs, then the home counties, then going (with new bills and a more pious style of "ad") into Wales, a great field always for a new patent medicine, and then into Lancashire. My uncle had in his inner office a big map of England, and as we took up fresh sections of the local press and our consignments invaded new areas, flags for advertisements and pink underlines for orders showed our progress.

"The romance of modern commerce, George!" my uncle would say, rubbing his hands together and drawing in air through his teeth. "The romance of modern commerce, eh? Conquest. Province by province."

We subjugated England and Wales; we rolled over the Cheviots with a special adaptation containing 11 percent of absolute alcohol; "Tono-Bungay: Thistle Brand." We also had the Fog poster adapted to a kilted Briton in a misty Highland scene.

Under the shadow of our great leading line we were presently taking subsidiary specialties into action; "Tono-Bungay Hair Stimulant" was our first supplement. Then came "Concentrated Tono-Bungay" for the eyes. That didn't go, but we had a considerable success with the Hair Stimulant. We broached the subject, I remember, in a little catechism beginning: "Why does the hair fall out? Because the follicles are fagged. What are the follicles?..." So it went on to the climax that the Hair Stimulant contained all "The essential principles of that most reviving tonic, Tono-Bungay, together with an emollient and nutritious oil derived from crude

Neat's Foot Oil by a process of refinement, separation, and deodorization.... It will be manifest to anyone of scientific attainments that in Neat's Foot Oil, derived from the hoofs and horns of beasts, we must necessarily have a *natural* skin and hair lubricant."

And we also did admirable things with our next subsidiaries, "Tono-Bungay Lozenges" and "Tono-Bungay Chocolate." These we urged upon the public for their extraordinary nutritive and recuperative value in cases of fatigue and strain. We gave them posters and illustrated advertisements showing climbers hanging from marvelously vertical cliffs, cyclist champions upon the track, mounted messengers engaged in Aix-to-Ghent rides, soldiers lying out in action under a hot sun. "You can GO for 24 hours," we declared, "on Tono-Bungay Chocolate." We didn't say whether you could return on the same commodity. We also showed a dreadfully barristerish barrister, wig, side-whiskers, teeth, a horribly lifelike portrait of all existing barristers, talking at a table, and beneath, this legend: "A Four Hours' Speech on Tono-Bungay Lozenges, and as fresh as when he began." That brought in regiments of school teachers, revivalist ministers, politicians, and the like. I really do believe there was an element of "kick" in the strychnine in these lozenges, especially in those made according to our earlier formula. For we altered all our formulae — invariably weakening them enormously as sales got ahead.

In a little while — so it seems to me now — we were employing travelers and opening up Great Britian at the rate of a hundred square miles a day. All the organization throughout was sketched in a crude, entangled, half-inspired fashion by my uncle, and all of it had to be worked out into a practicable scheme of quantities and expenditure by me. We had a lot of trouble finding our travelers; in the end at least half of them were Irish-Americans, a wonderful breed for selling medicine. We had still more trouble over our factory manager, because of the secrets of the inner room, and in the end we got a very capable woman, Mrs. Hampton Diggs, who had formerly managed a large millinery workroom, whom we could trust to keep everything in good working order without finding out anything that wasn't put exactly under her loyal and energetic nose. She conceived a high opinion of Tono-Bungay and took it in all forms and large quantities so long as I knew her. It didn't seem to do her any harm. And she kept the girls going quite wonderfully.

My uncle's last addition to the Tono-Bungay group was the Tono-Bungay Mouthwash. The reader has probably read a hundred times that inspiring inquiry of his, "You are Young Yet, but are you Sure Nothing has Aged your Gums?"

And after that we took over the agency for three or four good American lines that worked in with our own, and could be handled with it; "Texan Embrocation," and "23 — to clear the system" were the chief....

I set down these bare facts. To me they are all linked with the figure of my uncle. In some of the old 17th- and early 18th-century prayer books at Bladesover there used to be illustrations with long scrolls coming out of the mouths of the woodcut figures. I wish I could write all this last chapter on a scroll coming out of the head of my uncle, show it all the time as unfolding and pouring out from a short, fattening, small-legged man with stiff cropped hair, disobedient glasses on a perky little nose, and a round stare behind them. I wish I could show you him breathing hard and a little through his nose as his pen scribbled out some absurd inspiration for a poster or a picture page, and make you hear his voice, charged with solemn import like the voice of a squeaky prophet, saying, "George! list'n! I got an ideer. I got a notion, George!"

I should put myself into the same picture. Best setting for us, I think, would be the Beckenham snuggery, because there we worked hardest. It would be the lamplit room of the early '90's, and the clock upon the mantel would indicate midnight or later. We would be sitting on either side of the fire, I with a pipe, my uncle with a cigar or cigarette. There would be glasses standing inside the brass fender. Our expressions would be very grave. My uncle used to sit right back in his armchair; his toes always turned in when he was sitting down and his legs had a way of looking curved, as though they hadn't bones or joints but were stuffed with sawdust.

"George, whad'yer think of T.B. for seasickness?" he would say.

"No good that I can imagine."

"Oom! No harm *trying*, George. We can but try."

I would suck my pipe. "Hard to get at. Unless we sold our stuff specially at the docks. Might do a special at Cooks's office, or in the Continental Bradshaw."

"It' 'ud give 'em confidence, George."

He would Zzzz, with his glasses reflecting the red of the glowing coals.

"No good hiding our light under a Bushel," he would remark. . . .

I never really determined whether my uncle regarded Tono-Bungay as a fraud, or whether he didn't come to believe in it in a kind of way by the mere reiteration of his own assertions. I think that his average attitude was one of kindly, almost parental, toleration. I remember saying on one occasion, "But you don't suppose this stuff ever did a human being the slightest good at all?" and how his face assumed a look of protest, as of one reproving harshness and dogmatism.

"You've a hard nature, George," he said. "Yore're too ready to run things down. How can one *tell*? How can one venture to *tell*?..."

"The Brains" by Thomas Nast. The Metropolitan Museum of Art, New York.

Forenoon of an Honest Financial Racketeer

by Sinclair Lewis

His morning was not sharply marked into divisions. Interwoven with correspondence and advertisement-writing were a thousand nervous details: Calls from clerks who were incessantly and hopefully seeking five furnished rooms and bath at 60 dollars a month; advice to Mat Penniman on getting money out of tenants who had no money.

Babbitt's virtues as a real-estate broker — as the servant of society in the department of finding homes for families and shops for distributors of food — were steadiness and diligence. He was conventionally honest, he kept his records of buyers and sellers complete, he had experience with leases and titles and an excellent memory for prices. His shoulders were broad enough, his voice deep enough, his relish of hearty humor strong enough, to establish him as one of the ruling caste of Good Fellows. Yet his eventual importance to mankind was perhaps lessened by his large and complacent ignorance of all architecture save the types of houses turned out by speculative builders; all landscape gardening save the use of curving roads, grass, and six ordinary shrubs; and all the commonest axioms of economics. He serenely believed that the one purpose of the real-estate business was to make money for George F. Babbitt. True, it was a good advertisement at Boosters' Club lunches, and all the varieties of Annual Banquets to which Good Fellows were invited, to speak sonorously of Unselfish Public Service, the Broker's Obligation to Keep Inviolate the Trust of His Clients, and a thing called Ethics, whose nature was confusing but if you had it you were a High-Class Realtor and if you hadn't you were a shyster, a piker, and a fly-by-night. These virtues awakened Confidence, and enabled you to handle Bigger Propositions. But they didn't imply that you were to be impractical and refuse to take twice the value of a house if a buyer was such an idiot that he didn't haggle you down on the asking price.

Babbitt spoke well — and often — at these orgies of commercial righteousness about the "realtor's function as a seer of the future development of the community, and as a prophetic engineer clearing the pathway for inevitable changes" — which meant that a real-estate broker could make money by guessing which way the town would grow. This guessing he called Vision.

In an address at the Boosters' Club he had admitted, "It is at once the duty and the privilege of the realtor to know everything about his own city and its environs. Where a surgeon is a specialist on every vein and mysterious cell of the human body, and the engineer upon electricity in all its phases, or every bolt of some great bridge majestically arching o'er a mighty flood, the realtor must know his city, inch by inch, and all its faults and virtues."

Though he did know the market price, inch by inch, of certain districts of Zenith, he did not know whether the police force was too large or too small, or whether it was in alliance with gambling and prostitution. He knew the means of fireproofing buildings and the relation of insurance rates to fireproofing, but he did not know how many firemen there were in the city, how they were trained and paid, or how complete their apparatus. He sang eloquently the advantages of proximity of school buildings to rentable homes, but he did not know — he did not know that it was worthwhile to know — whether the city schoolrooms were properly heated, lighted, ventilated, furnished; he did not know how the teachers were chosen; and though he chanted, "One of the boasts of Zenith is that we pay our teachers adequately," that was because he had read the statement in the *Advocate-Times*. Himself, he could not have given the average salary of teachers in Zenith or anywhere else.

He had heard it said that "conditions" in the County Jail and the Zenith City Prison were not very "scientific"; he had, with indignation at the criticism of Zenith, skimmed through a report in which the notorious pessimist Seneca Doane, the radical lawyer, asserted that to throw boys and young girls into a bullpen crammed with men suffering from syphilis, delirium tremens, and insanity was not the perfect way of educating them. He had controverted the report by growling, "Folks that think a jail ought to be a bloomin' Hotel Thornleigh make me sick. If people don't like a jail, let 'em behave 'emselves and keep out of it. Besides, these reform cranks always exaggerate." That was the beginning and quite completely the end of his investigations into Zenith's charities and corrections....

As to industrial conditions, however, Babbitt had thought a great deal and his opinions may be coordinated as follows:

"A good labor union is of value because it keeps out radical unions, which would destroy property. No one ought to be forced to belong to a union however. All labor agitators who try to force men to join a union should be hanged. In fact, just between ourselves, there oughtn't to be any unions allowed at all; and as it's the best way of fighting the unions, every businessman ought to belong to an employers' association and to the Chamber of Commerce. In union there is strength. So any selfish hog who doesn't join the Chamber of Commerce ought to be forced to."

In nothing — as the expert on whose advice families moved to new neighborhoods to live there for a generation — was Babbitt more splendidly innocent than in the science of sanitation. He did not know a malaria-bearing mosquito from a bat; he knew nothing about tests of drinking water; and in the matters of plumbing and sewage he was as unlearned as he was voluble. He often referred to the excellence of the bathrooms in the houses he sold. He was fond of explaining why it was that no European ever bathed. Someone had told him, when he was 22, that all cesspools were unhealthy, and he still denounced them. If a client impertinently wanted him to sell a house which had a cesspool, Babbitt always spoke about it — before accepting the house and selling it.

When he laid out the Glen Oriole acreage development, when he ironed woodland and dipping meadow into a glenless, orioleless, sunburned flat prickly with small boards displaying the names of imaginary streets, he righteously put in a complete sewage system. It made him feel superior; it enabled him to sneer privily at the Martin Lumsen development, Avonlea, which had a cesspool; and it provided a chorus for the full-page advertisements in which he announced the beauty, convenience, cheapness, and superogatory healthfulness of Glen Oriole. The only flaw was that the Glen Oriole sewers had insufficient outlet, so that waste remained in them, not very agreeably, while the Avonlea cesspool was a Waring septic tank.

The whole of the Glen Oriole project was a suggestion that Babbitt, though he really did hate men recognized as swindlers, was not too unreasonably honest. Operators and buyers prefer that brokers should not be in competition with them as operators and buyers themselves, but attend to their clients' interests only. It was supposed that the Babbitt-Thompson Company were merely agents for Glen Oriole, serving the real owner, Jake Offutt, but the fact was that Babbitt and Thompson owned 62 percent of the Glen, the president and purchasing agent of the Zenith Street Traction Company owned 28 percent, and Jake Offutt (a gang politician, a small manufacturer, a tobacco-chewing old farceur who enjoyed dirty politics, business diplomacy, and cheating at poker) had only 10 percent, which Babbitt and the Traction officials had given to him for "fixing" health inspectors and fire inspectors and a member of the State Transportation Commission.

But Babbitt was virtuous. He advocated, though he did not practice, the prohibition of alcohol; he praised, though he did not obey, the laws against motor speeding; he paid his debts; he contributed to the church, the Red Cross, and the YMCA; he followed the custom of his clan and cheated only as it was sanctified by precedent; and he never descended to trickery — though, as he explained to Paul Riesling;

"Course I don't mean to say that every ad I write is literally true or that I always believe everything I say when I give some buyer a good strong selling spiel. You see — you see it's like this: In the first place, maybe the owner of the property exaggerated when he put it into my hands, and it certainly isn't my place to go proving my principal a liar! And then most folks are so darn crooked themselves that they expect a fellow to do a little lying, so if I was fool enough to never whoop the ante I'd get the credit for lying anyway! In self-defense I got to toot my own horn, like a lawyer defending a client — his bounden duty, ain't it, to bring out the poor dub's good points? Why, the Judge himself would bawl out a lawyer that didn't, even if they both knew the guy was guilty! But even so, I don't pad out the truth like Cecil Rountree or Thayer or the rest of these realtors. Fact, I think a fellow that's willing to deliberately up and profit by lying ought to be shot!"

Babbitt's value to his clients was rarely better shown than this morning, in the conference at 11:30 between himself, Conrad Lyte, and Archibald Purdy.

Conrad Lyte was a real-estate speculator. He was a nervous speculator. Before he gambled he consulted bankers, lawyers, architects, contracting builders, and all of their clerks and stenographers who were willing to be cornered and give him advice. He was a bold entrepreneur, and he desired nothing more than complete safety in his investments, freedom from attention to details, and the 30 or 40 percent profit which, according to all authorities, a pioneer deserves for his risks and foresight. He was a stubby man with a caplike mass of short gray curls and clothes which, no matter how well cut, seemed shaggy. Below his eyes were semicircular hollows, as though silver dollars had been pressed against them and had left an imprint.

Particularly and always Lyte consulted Babbitt,

and trusted in his slow cautiousness.

Six months ago Babbitt had learned that one Archibald Purdy, a grocer in the indecisive residential district known as Linton, was talking of opening a butcher shop beside his grocery. Looking up the ownership of adjoining parcels of land, Babbitt found that Purdy owned his present shop but did not own the one available lot adjoining. He advised Conrad Lyte to purchase this lot for 11,000 dollars, though an appraisal on a basis of rents did not indicate its value as above 9,000. The rents, declared Babbitt, were too low; and by waiting they could make Purdy come to their price. (This was Vision.) He had to bully Lyte into buying. His first act as agent for Lyte was to increase the rent of the battered store building on the lot. The tenant said a number of rude things, but he paid.

Now Purdy seemed ready to buy, and his delay was going to cost him 10,000 extra dollars — the reward paid by the community to Mr. Conrad Lyte for the virtue of employing a broker who had Vision and who understood Talking Points, Strategic Values, Key Situations, Underappraisals, and the Psychology of Salesmanship.

Lyte came to the conference exultantly. He was fond of Babbitt this morning, and called him "old hoss." Purdy, the grocer, a long-nosed man and solemn, seemed to care less for Babbitt and for Vision, but Babbitt met him at the street door of the office and guided him toward the private room with affectionate little cries of "This way, Brother Purdy!" He took from the correspondence file the entire box of cigars and forced them on his guests. He pushed their chairs two inches forward and three inches back, which gave a hospitable note, then leaned back in his desk chair and looked plump and jolly. But he spoke to the weakling grocer with firmness.

"Well, Brother Purdy, we been having some pretty tempting offers from butchers and a slew of other folks for that lot next to your store, but I persuaded Brother Lyte that we ought to give you a shot at the property first. I said to Lyte, 'It'd be a rotten shame,' I -said, 'if somebody went and opened a combination grocery and meat market right next door and ruined Purdy's nice little business.' Especially — " Babbitt leaned forward, and his voice was harsh, " — it would be hard luck if one of these cash-and-carry chain stores got in there and started cutting prices below cost till they got rid of competition and forced you to the wall!"

Purdy snatched his thin hands from his pockets, pulled up his trousers, thrust his hands back into his pockets, tilted in the heavy oak chair, and tried to look amused, as he struggled:

"Yes, they're bad competition. But I guess you don't realize the Pulling Power that Personality has in a neighborhood business."

The great Babbitt smiled. "That's so. Just as you feel, old man. We thought we'd give you first chance. All right then — "

"Now look here!" Purdy wailed. "I know f'r a fact that a piece of property 'bout same size, right near, sold for less 'n 8,500, 'twa'n't two years ago, and here you fellows are asking me 24,000 dollars! Why, I'd have to mortgage — I wouldn't mind so much paying 12,000 but — Why good God, Mr. Babbit, you're asking more 'n twice its value! And threatening to ruin me if I don't take it!"

"Purdy, I don't like your way of talking! I don't like it one little bit! Supposing Lyte and I were stinking enough to want to ruin any fellow human, don't you suppose we know it's to our own selfish interest to have everybody in Zenith prosperous? But all this is beside the point. Tell you what we'll do: We'll come down to 23,000 — 5,000 down and the rest on mortgage — and if you want to wreck the old shack and rebuild, I guess I can get Lyte here to loosen up for a building mortgage on good liberal terms. Heavens, man, we'd be glad to oblige you! We don't like these foreign grocery trusts any better 'n you do! But it isn't reasonable to expect us to sacrifice 11,000 or more just for neighborliness, *is* it! How about it, Lyte? You willing to come down?"

By warmly taking Purdy's part, Babbitt persuaded the benevolent Mr. Lyte to reduce his price to 21,000 dollars. At the right moment Babbitt snatched from a drawer the agreement he had Miss McGoun type out a week ago and thrust it into Purdy's hands. He genially shook his fountain pen to make certain that it was flowing, handed it to Purdy, and approvingly watched him sign.

The work of the world was being done. Lyte had made something over 9,000 dollars; Babbitt had made a 450 dollar commission; Purdy had, by the sensitive mechanism of modern finance, been provided with a business building; and soon the happy inhabitants of Linton would have meat lavished upon them at prices only a little higher than those downtown.

It had been a manly battle, but after it Babbitt drooped. This was the only really amusing contest he had been planning. There was nothing ahead save details of leases, appraisals, mortgages.

He muttered, "Makes me sick to think of Lyte carrying off most of the profit when I did all the work, the old skinflint! And — what else have I got to do today?...Like to take a good long vacation. Motor trip. Something."

Ballad of the Landlord

Landlord, landlord,
My roof has sprung a leak
Don't you 'member I told you about it
Way last week?

Landlord, landlord,
These steps is broken down.
When you come up yourself
It's a wonder you don't fall down.

Ten Bucks you say I owe you?
Ten Bucks you say is due?
Well, that's Ten Bucks more'n I'll pay you
Till you fix this house up new.

What? You gonna get eviction orders?
You gonna cut off my heat?
You gonna take my furniture and
Throw it in the street?

Um-huh! You talking high and mighty.
Talk on — till you get through.
You ain't gonna be able to say a word
If I land my fist on you.

Police! Police!
Come and get this man!
He's trying to ruin the government
And overturn the land!

Copper's whistle!
Patrol bell!
Arrest.

Precinct Station.
Iron cell.
Headlines in press:

MAN THREATENS LANDLORD

TENANT HELD NO BAIL

JUDGE GIVES NEGRO 90 DAYS IN COUNTY
  JAIL

Langston Hughes

5.War

HMM...

WHAT WOULD YOU DO IF I PUSHED YOUR SNOWMAN OVER?

NOTHING... WHAT **COULD** I DO?

YOU'RE BIGGER AND STRONGER THAN I AM... YOU'RE OLDER...YOU CAN RUN FASTER... I REALLY COULDN'T DO ANYTHING TO STOP YOU

I REALIZE FULL WELL THAT I AM AT YOUR MERCY WHERE THINGS OF THIS SORT ARE CONCERNED...ALL I CAN DO IS SIMPLY HOPE THAT YOU WILL CHOOSE NOT TO DO SO...

LITTLE BY LITTLE I'M BECOMING AN EXPERT AT THE SOFT ANSWER..

The Toys of Peace

by Saki

"Harvey," said Eleanor Bope, handing her brother a cutting from a London morning paper of the 19th of March, "just read this about children's toys, please; it exactly carries out some of our ideas about influence and upbringing."

"In the view of the National Peace Council," ran the extract, "there are grave objections to presenting our boys with regiments of fighting men, batteries of guns, and squadrons of 'Dreadnoughts.' Boys, the Council admits, naturally love fighting and all the panoply of war...but that is no reason for encouraging, and perhaps giving permanent form to, their primitive instincts. At the Children's Welfare Exhibition, which opens at Olympia in three weeks' time, the Peace Council will make an alternative suggestion to parents in the shape of an exhibition of 'peace toys.' In front of a specially painted representation of the Peace Palace at The Hague will be grouped, not miniature soliders but miniature civilians, not guns but ploughs and the tools of industry....It is hoped that manufacturers may take a hint from the exhibit, which will bear fruit in the toy shops."

"The idea is certainly an interesting and very well-meaning one," said Harvey; "whether it would succeed well in practice — "

"We must try," interrupted his sister; "you are coming down to us at Easter, and you always bring the boys some toys, so that will be an excellent opportunity for you to inaugurate the new experiment. Go about in the shops and buy any little toys and models that have special bearing on civilian life in its more peaceful aspects. Of course you must explain the toys to the children and interest them in the new idea. I regret to say that the 'Siege of Adrianople' toy, that their Aunt Susan sent them, didn't need any explanation; they knew all the uniforms and flags, and even the names of the respective commanders, and when I heard them one day using what seemed to be the most objectionable language, they said it was Bulgarian words of command; of course it *may* have been, but at any rate I took the toy away from them. Now I shall expect your Easter gifts to give quite a new impulse and direction to the children's minds; Eric is not eleven yet, and Bertie is only nine and one-half, so they are really at a most impressionable age."

"There is primitive instinct to be taken into consideration, you know," said Harvey doubtfully, "and hereditary tendencies as well. One of their great-uncles fought in the most intolerant fashion at Inkerman — he was specially mentioned in dispatches, I believe — and their great-grandfather smashed all his Whig neighbors' hothouses when the great Reform Bill was passed. Still, as you say, they are at an impressionable age. I will do my best."

On Easter Saturday Harvey Bope unpacked a large, promising-looking red cardboard box under the expectant eyes of his nephews. "Your uncle has brought you the newest thing in toys," Eleanor had said impressively, and youthful anticipation had been anxiously divided between Albanian soldiery and a Somali camel corps. Eric was hotly in favor of the latter contingency. "There would be Arabs on horseback," he whispered; "the Albanians have got jolly uniforms, and they fight all day long, and all night too, when there's a moon, but the country's rocky, so they've got no cavalry."

A quantity of crinkly paper shavings was the first thing that met the view when the lid was removed; the most exciting toys always began like that. Harvey pushed back the top layer and drew forth a square, rather featureless building.

"It's a fort!" exclaimed Bertie.

"It isn't, it's the palace of the Mpret of Albania," said Eric, immensely proud of his knowledge of the exotic title; "It's got no windows, you see, so that passersby can't fire in at the Royal Family."

"It's a municipal dustbin," said Harvey hurriedly; "You see all the refuse and litter of a town is collected there, instead of lying about and injuring the health of the citizens."

In an awful silence he disinterred a little lead figure of a man in black clothes.

"That," he said, "is a distinguished civilian, John Stuart Mill. He was an authority on political economy."

"Why?" asked Bertie.

"Well, he wanted to be; he thought it was a useful thing to be."

Bertie gave an expressive grunt, which conveyed his opinion that there was no accounting for tastes.

Another square building came out, this time with windows and chimneys.

"A model of the Manchester branch of the Young Women's Christian Association," said Harvey.

"Are there any lions?" asked Eric hopefully. He had been reading Roman history and thought that where you found Christians you might reasonably expect to find a few lions.

"There are no lions," said Harvey. "Here is another civilian, Robert Raikes, the founder of Sunday schools, and here is a model of a municipal washhouse. These little round things are loaves baked in a sanitary bakehouse. That lead figure is a sanitary inspector, this one is a district councillor, and this one is an official of the Local Government Board."

"What does he do?" asked Eric wearily.

"He sees to things connected with his department," said Harvey. "This box with a slit in it is a ballot box. Votes are put into it at election times."

"What is put into it at other times?" asked Bertie.

"Nothing. And here are some tools of industry, a wheelbarrow and a hoe, and I think these are meant for hop poles. This is a model beehive, and that is a ventilator, for ventilating sewers. This seems to be another municipal dustbin — no, it is a model of a school of art and a public library. This little lead figure is Mrs. Hemans, a poetess, and this is Rowland Hill, who introduced the system of penny postage. This is Sir John Herschel, the eminent astrologer."

"Are we to play with these civilian figures?" asked Eric.

"Of course," said Harvey, "these are toys; they are meant to be played with."

"But how?"

It was rather a poser. "You might make two of them contest a seat in Parliament," said Harvey, "and have an election — "

"With rotten eggs, and free fights, and ever so many broken heads!" exclaimed Eric.

"And noses all bleeding and everybody drunk as can be," echoed Bertie, who had carefully studied one of Hogarth's pictures.

"Nothing of the kind," said Harvey, "nothing in the least like that. Votes will be put in the ballot box, and the mayor will count them — the district councillor will do for the mayor — and he will say which has received the most votes, and then the two candidates will thank him for presiding, and each will say that the contest has been conducted throughout in the pleasantest and most straightforward fashion, and they part with expressions of mutual esteem. There's a jolly game for you boys to play. I never had such toys when I was young."

"I don't think we'll play with them just now," said Eric, with an entire absence of the enthusiasm that his uncle had shown; "I think perhaps we ought to do a little of our holiday task. It's history this time; we've got to learn up something about the Bourbon period in France."

"The Bourbon period," said Harvey, with some disapproval in his voice.

"We've got to know something about Louis XIV," continued Eric; "I've learned the names of all the principal battles already."

This would never do. "There were, of course, some battles fought during his reign," said Harvey, "but I fancy the accounts of them were much exaggerated; news was very unreliable in those days, and there were practically no war correspondents, so generals and commanders could magnify every little skirmish they engaged in till they reached the proportions of decisive battles. Louis was really famous, now, as a landscape gardener; the way he laid out Versailles was so much admired that it was copied all over Europe."

"Do you know anything about Madame Du Barry?" asked Eric; "didn't she have her head chopped off?"

"She was another great lover of gardening," said Harvey evasively; "in fact, I believe the well-known rose Du Barry was named after her, and now I think you had better play for a little and leave your lessons till later."

Harvey retreated to the library and spent some 30 or 40 minutes in wondering whether it would be possible to compile a history, for use in elementary schools, in which there should be no prominent mention of battles, massacres, murderous intrigues, and violent deaths. The York and Lancaster period and the Napoleonic era would, he admitted to himself, present considerable difficulties, and the Thirty Years' War would entail something of a gap if you left it out altogether. Still, it would be something gained if, at a highly impressionable age, children could be got to fix their attention on the invention of calico printing instead of the Spanish Armada or the Battle of Waterloo.

It was time, he thought, to go back to the boys' room, and see how they were getting on with their peace toys. As he stood outside the door he could hear Eric's voice raised in command; Bertie chimed in now and again with a helpful suggestion.

"That is Louis XIV," Eric was saying, "that one in knee breeches, that Uncle said invented Sunday schools. It isn't a bit like him, but it'll have to do."

"We'll give him a purple coat from my paintbox by and by," said Bertie.

"Yes, an' red heels. That is Madame de Maintenon, that one he called Mrs. Hemans. She begs

Louis not to go on this expedition, but he turns a deaf ear. He takes Marshal Saxe with him, and we must pretend that they have thousands of men with them. The watchword is *Qui vive?* and the answer is *L'etat c'est moi* — that was one of his favorite remarks, you know. They land at Manchester in the dead of night, and a Jacobite conspirator gives them the keys of the fortress.''

Peeping in through the doorway Harvey observed that the municipal dustbin had been pierced with holes to accommodate the muzzles of imaginary cannons, and now represented the principal fortified position in Manchester; John Stuart Mill had been dipped in red ink, and apparently stood for Marshal Saxe.

"Louis orders his troops to surround the Young Women's Christian Association and seize the lot of them. 'Once back at the Louvre and the girls are mine,' he exclaims. We must use Mrs. Hemans again for one of the girls; she says 'Never,' and stabs Marshal Saxe in the heart.''

"He bleeds dreadfully," exclaimed Bertie, splashing red ink liberally over the facade of the Association building.

"The soldiers rush in and avenge his death with the utmost savagery. A hundred girls are killed" — here Bertie emptied the remainder of the red ink over the Association building — "and the surviving 500 are dragged off to the French ships. 'I have lost a marshal,' says Louis, 'but I do not go back empty-handed.' ''

Harvey stole away from the room, and sought out his sister.

"Eleanor," he said, "the experiment — ''

"Yes?''

"Has failed. We have begun too late.''

The War Prayer

by Mark Twain

It was a time of great and exalting excitement. The country was up in arms, the war was on, in every breast burned the holy fire of patriotism; the drums were beating, the bands playing, the toy pistols popping, the bunched firecrackers hissing and spluttering; on every hand and far down the receding and fading spread of roofs and balconies a fluttering wilderness of flags flashed in the sun; daily the young volunteers marched down the wide avenue gay and fine in their new uniforms, the proud fathers and mothers and sisters and sweethearts cheering them with voices choked with happy emotion as they swung by; nightly the packed mass meetings listened, panting, to patriot oratory which stirred the deepest deeps of their hearts, and which they interrupted at briefest intervals with cyclones of applause, the tears running down their cheeks the while; in the churches the pastors preached devotion to flag and country, and invoked the God of Battles, beseeching His aid in our good cause in outpouring of fervid eloquence which moved every listener. It was indeed a glad and gracious time, and the half dozen rash spirits that ventured to disapprove of the war and cast a doubt upon its righteousness straightway got such a stern and angry warning that for their personal safety's sake they quickly shrank out of sight and offended no more in that way.

Sunday morning came — next day the battalions would leave for the front; the church was filled; the volunteers were there, their young faces alight with martial dreams — visions of the stern advance, the gathering momentum, the rushing charge, the flashing sabers, the flight of the foe, the tumult, the enveloping smoke, the fierce pursuit, the surrender! — then home from the war, bronzed heroes, welcomed, adored, submerged in golden seas of glory! With the volunteers sat their dear ones, proud, happy, and envied by the neighbors and friends who had no sons and brothers to send forth to the field of honor, there to win for the flag or, failing, die the noblest of noble deaths. The service proceeded; a war chapter from the Old Testament was read; the first prayer was said; it was followed by an organ burst that shook the building, and with one impulse the house rose, with glowing eyes and beating hearts, and poured out that tremendous invocation —

"God the all-terrible! Thou who ordainest,
Thunder thy clarion and lightning thy sword!"

Then came the "long" prayer. None could remember the like of it for passionate pleading and moving and beautiful language. The burden of its supplication was, that an ever-merciful and benignant Father of us all would watch over our noble young soldiers, and aid, comfort, and encourage them in their patriotic work; bless them, shield them in the day of battle and the hour of peril, bear them in His mighty hand, make them strong and confident, invincible in the bloody onset; help them to crush the foe, grant to them and to their flag and country imperishable honor and glory —

An aged stranger entered and moved with slow and noiseless step up the main aisle, his eyes fixed upon the minister, his long body clothed in a robe that reached to his feet, his head bare, his white hair descending in a frothy cataract to his shoulders, his seamy face unnaturally pale, pale even to ghastliness. With all eyes following him and wondering, he made his silent way; without pausing, he ascended to the preacher's side and stood there, waiting. With shut lids the preacher, unconscious of his presence, continued his moving prayer, and at last finished it with the words, uttered in fervent appeal, "Bless our arms, grant us the victory, Oh Lord our God, Father and Protector of our land and flag!"

The stranger touched his arm, motioned him to step aside — which the startled minister did — and took his place. During some moments he surveyed the spellbound audience with solemn eyes, in which burned an uncanny light; then in a deep voice he said:

"I come from the Throne — bearing a message from Almighty God!" The words smote the house with a shock; if the stranger perceived it he gave no attention. "He has heard the prayer of His servant your shepherd, and will grant it if such shall be your desire after I, His messenger, shall have explained to you its import — that is to say, its full import. For it is like unto many of the prayers of men, in that it asks for more than he who utters it is aware of — except he pause and think.

"God's servant and yours has prayed his prayer. Has he paused and taken thought? Is it one prayer? No, it is two — one uttered, the other not. Both have reached the ear of Him Who heareth all supplications, the spoken and the unspoken. Ponder this — keep it in mind. If you would beseech a blessing upon yourself, beware! least without intent you invoke a curse upon a neighbor at the same time. If you pray for the blessing of rain upon your crop which needs it, by that act you are possibly praying for a curse upon some neighbor's crop which may not need rain and can be injured by it.

"You have heard your servant's prayer — the uttered part of it. I am commissioned of God to put into words the other part of it — that part which the pastor — and also you in your hearts — fervently prayed silently. And ignorantly and unthinkingly? God grant that it was so! You heard these words: 'Grant us the victory, Oh Lord our God!' That is sufficient. The *whole* of the uttered prayer is compact into those pregnant words. Elaborations were not necessary. When you have prayed for victory you have prayed for many unmentioned results which follow victory — *must* follow it, cannot help but follow it. Upon the listening spirit of God the Father fell also the unspoken part of the prayer. He commandeth me to put it into our words. Listen!

"Oh Lord our Father, our young patriots, idols of our hearts, go forth to battle — be Thou near them! With them — in spirit — we also go forth from the sweet peace of our beloved firesides to smite the foe. Oh Lord our God, help us to tear their soldiers to bloody shreds with our shells; help us to cover their smiling fields with the pale forms of their patriot dead; help us to drown the thunder of the guns with the shrieks of their wounded, writhing in pain; help us to lay waste their humble homes with a hurricane of fire; help us to wring the hearts of their unoffending widows with unavailing grief; help us to turn them out roofless with their little children to wander unfriended the wastes of their desolated land in rags and hunger and thirst, sports of the sun flames of summer and the icy winds of winter, broken in spirit, worn with travail, imploring Thee for the refuge of the grave and denied it — for our sakes who adore Thee, Lord, blast their hopes, blight their lives, protract their bitter pilgrimage, make heavy their steps, water their way with their tears, stain the white snow with the blood of their wounded feet! We ask it, in the spirit of love, of Him Who is the Source of Love, and Who is the ever-faithful Refuge and Friend of all that are sore beset and seek His aid with humble and contrite hearts. Amen."

(After a pause.) "Ye have prayed it; if ye still desire it, speak! The messenger of the Most High waits."

It was believed afterward that the man was a lunatic, because there was no sense in what he said.

The Heroes

I dreamed of war heroes, of wounded war heroes
With just enough of their charms shot away
To make them more handsome. The women moved
    nearer
To touch their brave wounds and their hair streaked
    with gray.

I saw them in long ranks ascending the gangplanks;
The girls with the doughnuts were cheerful and gay.
They minded their manners and muttered their
    thanks;
The chaplain advised them to watch and to pray.

They shipped these rapscallions, these seasick battal-
    ions
To a patriotic and picturesque spot;
They gave them new Bibles and marksmen's medal-
    lions,
Compasses, maps, and committed the lot.

A fine dust has settled on all that scrap metal.
The heroes were packaged and sent home in parts
To pluck at a poppy and sew on a petal
And count the long night by the stroke of their
    hearts.

Louis Simpson

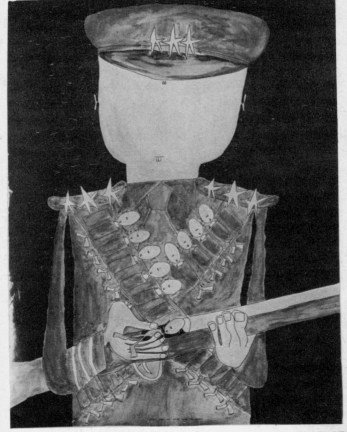

From PROP ART

© 1972 Gary Yanker

Knowlt Hoheimer

I was the first fruits of the battle of Missionary
   Ridge.
When I felt the bullet enter my heart
I wished I had stayed at home and gone to jail
For stealing the hogs of Curl Trenary,
Instead of running away and joining the army.
Rather a thousand times the county jail
Then to lie under this marble figure with wings,
And this granite pedestal
Bearing the words, "Pro Patria."
What do they mean, anyway?

Edgar Lee Masters

From Catch-22

by Joseph Heller

Doc Daneeka didn't laugh until Yossarian came to him one mission later and pleaded again, without any real expectation of success, to be grounded. Doc Daneeka snickered once and was soon immersed in problems of his own, which included Chief White Halfoat, who had been challenging him all that morning to Indian wrestle, and Yossarian, who decided right then and there to go crazy.

"You're wasting your time," Doc Daneeka was forced to tell him.

"Can't you ground someone who's crazy?"

"Oh, sure. I have to. There's a rule saying I have to ground anyone who's crazy," said Doc Daneeka.

"Then why don't you ground me? I'm crazy. Ask Clevinger."

"Clevinger? Where *is* Clevinger? You find Clevinger and I'll ask him."

"Then ask any of the others. They'll tell you how crazy I am."

"They're crazy."

"Then why don't you ground them?"

"Why don't they ask me to ground them?"

"Because they're crazy, that's why."

"Of course they're crazy," Doc Daneeka replied. "I just told you they're crazy, didn't I? And you can't let crazy people decide whether you're crazy or not, can you?"

Yossarian looked at him soberly and tried another approach. "Is Orr crazy?"

"He sure is," Doc Daneeka said.

"Can you ground him?"

"I sure can. But first he has to ask me to. That's part of the rule."

"Then why doesn't he ask you to?"

"Because he's crazy," Doc Daneeka said. "He has to be crazy to keep flying combat missions after all the close calls he's had. Sure, I can ground Orr. But first he has to ask me to."

"That's all he has to do to be grounded?"

"That's all. Let him ask me."

"And then you can ground him?" Yossarian asked.

"No. Then I can't ground him."

"You mean there's a catch?"

"Sure there's a catch," Doc Daneeka replied. "Catch-22. Anyone who wants to get out of combat duty isn't really crazy."

There was only one catch and that was Catch-22, which specified that a concern for one's own safety in the face of dangers that were real and immediate was the process of a rational mind. Orr was crazy and could be grounded. All he had to do was ask; and as soon as he did, he would no longer be crazy and would have to fly more missions. Orr would be crazy to fly more missions and sane if he didn't, but if he was sane he had to fly them. If he flew them he was crazy and didn't have to; but if he didn't want to he was sane and had to. Yossarian was moved very deeply by the absolute simplicity of this clause of Catch-22 and let out a respectful whistle.

"That's some catch, that Catch-22," he observed.

"It's the best there is," Doc Daneeka agreed.

Yossarian saw it clearly in all its spinning reasonableness. There was an elliptical precision about its perfect pairs of parts that was graceful and shocking, like good modern art, and at times Yossarian wasn't quite sure that he saw it at all, just the way he was never quite sure about good modern art or about the flies Orr saw in Appleby's eyes. He had Orr's word to take for the flies in Appleby's eyes.

"Oh, they're there, all right," Orr had assured him about the flies in Appleby's eyes after Yossarian's fist fight with Appleby in the officers' club, "although he probably doesn't even know it. That's why he can't see things as they really are."

"How come he doesn't know it?" inquired Yossarian.

"Because he's got flies in his eyes," Orr explained with exaggerated patience. "How can he see he's got flies in his eyes if he's got flies in his eyes?"

It made as much sense as anything else, and Yossarian was willing to give Orr the benefit of the doubt because Orr was from the wilderness outside New York City and knew so much more about wildlife than Yossarian did, and because Orr, unlike Yossarian's mother, father, sister, brother, aunt, uncle, in-law, teacher, spiritual leader, legislator, neighbor, and newspaper, had never lied to him about anything crucial before. Yossarian had mulled his newfound knowledge about Appleby over in private for a day or two and then decided, as a good deed, to pass the word along to Appleby himself.

"Appleby, you've got flies in your eyes," he

whispered helpfully as they passed by each other in the doorway of the parachute tent on the day of the weekly milk run to Parma.

"What?" Appleby responded sharply, thrown into confusion by the fact that Yossarian had spoken to him at all.

"You've got flies in your eyes," Yossarian repeated. "That's probably why you can't see them."

Appleby retreated from Yossarian with a look of loathing bewilderment and sulked in silence until he was in the jeep with Havermeyer riding down the long straight road to the briefing room, where Major Danby, the fidgeting group operations officer, was waiting to conduct the preliminary briefing with all the lead pilots, bombardiers, and navigators. Appleby spoke in a soft voice so that he would not be heard by the driver or by Captain Black who was stretched out with his eyes closed in the front seat of the jeep.

"Havermeyer," he asked hesitantly. "Have I got flies in my eyes?"

Havermeyer blinked quizzically. "Sties?" he asked.

"No, flies," he was told.

Havermeyer blinked again. "Flies?"

"In my eyes."

"You must be crazy," Havermeyer said.

"No, I'm not crazy. Yossarian's crazy. Just tell me if I've got flies in my eyes or not. Go ahead. I can take it."

Havermeyer popped another piece of peanut brittle into his mouth and peered very closely into Appleby's eyes.

"I don't see any," he announced.

Appleby heaved an immense sigh of relief. Havermeyer had tiny bits of peanut brittle adhering to his lips, chin, and cheeks.

"You've got peanut-brittle crumbs on your face," Appleby remarked to him.

"I'd rather have peanut-brittle crumbs on my face than flies in my eyes," Havermeyer retorted.

The officers of the other five planes in each flight arrived in trucks for the general briefing that took place 30 minutes later. The three enlisted men in each crew were not briefed at all, but were carried directly out on the airfield to separate planes in which they were scheduled to fly that day, where they waited around with the ground crew until the officers with whom they had been scheduled to fly swung off the rattling tailgates of the trucks delivering them and it was time to climb aboard and start up. Engines rolled over disgruntledly on lollipop-shaped hardstands, resisting first, then idling smoothly awhile, and then the planes lumbered around and nosed forward lamely over the pebbled ground like sightless, stupid, crippled things until they taxied into the line at the foot of the landing strip and took off swiftly, one behind the other, in a zooming, rising roar, banking slowly into formation over mottled treetops, and circling the field at even speed until all the flights of six had been formed and then settling course over cerulean water on the first leg of the journey to the target in northern Italy or France. The planes gained altitude steadily and were above 9,000 feet by the time they crossed into enemy territory. One of the surprising things always was the sense of calm and utter silence, broken only by the test rounds fired from the machine guns, by an occasional toneless, terse remark over the intercom, and, at last, by the sobering pronouncement of the bombardier in each plane that they were at the I.P. and about to turn toward the target. There was always sunshine, always a tiny sticking in the throat from the rarefied air.

The B-25's they flew in were stable, dependable, dull-green ships with twin rudders and engines and wide wings. Their single fault, from where Yossarian sat as a bombardier, was the tight crawlway separating the bombardier's compartment in the Plexiglas nose from the nearest escape hatch. The crawlway was a narrow, square, cold tunnel hollowed out beneath the flight controls, and a large man like Yossarian could squeeze through only with difficulty. A chubby, moonfaced navigator with little reptilian eyes and a pipe like Aarfy's had trouble too, and Yossarian used to chase him back from the nose as they turned toward the target, now minutes away. There was a time of tension then, a time of waiting with nothing to hear and nothing to see and nothing to do but wait as the antiaircraft guns below took aim and made ready to knock them all sprawling into infinite sleep if they could.

The crawlway was Yossarian's lifeline to outside from a plane about to fall, but Yossarian swore at it with seething antagonism, reviled it as an obstacle put there by providence as part of the plot that would destroy him. There was room for an additional escape hatch right there in the nose of a B-25, but there was no escape hatch. Instead there was the crawlway, and since the mess on the mission over Avignon he had learned to detest every mammoth inch of it, for it slung him seconds and seconds away from his parachute, which was too bulky to be taken up front with him, and seconds and seconds more after that away from the escape hatch on the floor between the rear of the elevated flight deck and the feet of the faceless top turret gunner mounted high above. Yossarian longed to be where Aarfy could be once Yossarian had chased him back from the nose; Yossarian longed to sit on the floor in a huddled ball right on top of the escape hatch inside a sheltering igloo of extra flak suits that he would have been happy to carry along with him, his parachute already hooked to his harness where it belonged, one fist clenching the red-handled rip cord, one fist gripping the emergency hatch release that would spill him earthward into air at the first dreadful squeal of destruction. That was where he wanted to be if he had to be there at all, instead of hung out there in front like some cantilevered goldfish in some cantilevered goldfish bowl while the foul black tiers of flak were bursting and booming and billowing all around and above and below him in a climbing, cracking, staggered, banging, phantasmagorical, cosmological wickedness that jarred and tossed and shivered, clattered, and pierced, and threatened to annihilate them all in one splinter of a second in one vast flash of fire.

Aarfy had been no use to Yossarian as a navigator or as anything else, and Yossarian drove him back from the nose vehemently each time so that they would not clutter up each other's way if they had to scramble suddenly for safety. Once Yossarian had driven him back from the nose, Aarfy was free to cower on the floor where Yossarian longed to cower, but he stood bolt upright instead with his stumpy arms resting comfortable on the backs of the pilot's and copilot's seat, pipe in hand, making affable small talk to McWatt and whoever happened to be copilot and pointing out amusing trivia in the sky to the two men, who were too busy to be interested. McWatt was too busy responding at the controls to Yossarian's strident instructions as Yossarian slipped the plane in on the bomb run and then whipped them all away violently around the ravenous pillars of exploding shells with curt, shrill, obscene commands to McWatt that were much like the anguished, entreating nightmare yelpings of Hungry Joe in the dark. Aarfy would puff reflectively on his pipe throughout the whole chaotic clash, gazing with unruffled curiosity at the war through McWatt's window as though it were a remote disturbance that could not affect him. Aarfy was a dedicated fraternity man who loved cheerleading and class reunions and did not have brains enough to be afraid. Yossarian did have brains enough and was, and the only thing that stopped him from abandoning his post under fire and scurrying back through the crawlway like a yellow-bellied rat was his unwillingness to entrust the evasive action out of the target area to anybody else. There was nobody else in the world he would honor with so great a responsibility. There was nobody else he knew who was as big a coward. Yossarian was the best man in the group at evasive action, but had no idea why.

There was no established procedure for evasive action. All you needed was fear, and Yossarian had plenty of that, more fear than Orr or Hungry Joe, more fear even than Dunbar, who had resigned himself submissively to the idea that he must die some day. Yossarian had not resigned himself to that idea, and he bolted for his life wildly on each mission the instant his bombs were away, hollering, "*Hard, hard, hard, hard, hard!*" at McWatt and hating McWatt viciously all the time as though McWatt were to blame for their being up there at all to be rubbed out by strangers, and everybody else in the plane kept off the intercom, except for the pitiful time of the mess on the mission to Avignon when Dobbs went crazy in midair and began weeping pathetically for help.

"Help him, help him," Dobbs sobbed. "Help him, help him."

"Help who? Help who?" called back Yossarian, once he had plugged his headset back into the intercom system, after it had been jerked out when Dobbs wrested the controls away from Huple and hurled them all down suddenly into the deafening, paralyzing, horrifying dive which had plastered Yossarian helplessly to the ceiling of the plane by the top of his head and from which Huple had rescued them just in time by seizing the controls back from Dobbs and leveling their ship out almost as suddenly right back in the middle of the buffeting layer of cacophonous flak from which they had escaped successfully only a moment before. *Oh, God! Oh, God, oh, God*, Yossarian had been pleading wordlessly as he dangled from the ceiling of the nose of the ship by the top of his head, unable to move.

"The bombardier, the bombardier," Dobbs answered in a cry when Yossarian spoke. "He doesn't answer, he doesn't answer. Help the bombardier, help the bombardier."

"I'm the bombardier," Yossarian cried back at him. "I'm the bombardier. I'm all right. I'm all right."

"Then help him, help him," Dobbs begged. "Help him, help him."

And Snowden lay dying in back.

APO 96225

A young man once went off to war
in a far country.
When he had time, he wrote home and
said, "Sure rains here a lot."

But his mother, reading between the lines,
Wrote, "We're quite concerned. Tell us
what it's really like."

And the young man responded, "Wow, you ought
to see the funny monkeys!"

To which the mother replied, "Don't
hold back, how is it?"

And the young man wrote, "The sunsets here
are spectacular."

In her next letter the mother
wrote, "Son, we want you to tell us
everything."

So the next time he wrote,
"Today I killed a man.
Yesterday I helped drop napalm on women and
children. Tomorrow we are going to use gas."

And the father wrote, "Please don't
write such depressing letters. You're upsetting
your mother."

So, after a while, the young man wrote, "Sure rains a
lot here ...."

Larry Rottmann

War Is Kind

Do not weep, maiden, for war is kind.
Because your lover threw wild hands toward the sky
And the affrighted steed ran on alone,
Do not weep.
War is kind.

Hoarse, booming drums of the regiment,
Little souls who thirst for fight,
These men were born to drill and die.
The unexplained glory flies above them,
Great is the battle-god, great, and his
kingdom —
A field where a thousand corpses lie.

Do not weep, babe, for war is kind.
Because your father tumbled in the yellow trenches,
Raged at his breast, gulped, and died,
Do not weep.
War is kind.

Swift blazing flag of the regiment,
Eagle with crest of red and gold,
These men were born to drill and die.
Point for them the virtue of slaughter,
Make plain to them the excellence of killing
And a field where a thousand corpses lie.

Mother whose heart hung humble as a button
On the bright splendid shroud of your son,
Do not weep.
War is kind.

Stephen Crane

6.
The Sexes

"Happiness." Courtesy of the Brazilian Coffee Institute.

Symptoms of Love

Love is a universal migraine,
A bright stain on the vision
Blotting out reason.

Symptoms of true love
Are leanness, jealousy,
Laggard dawns;

Are omens and nightmares —
Listening for a knock,
Waiting for a sign:

For a touch of her fingers
In a darkened room,
For a searching look.

Take courage, lover!
Could you endure such pain
At any hand but hers?

Robert Graves

He and She

When I am dead you'll find it hard,
 Said he,
To ever find another man
 Like me.

What makes you think, as I suppose
 You do,
I'd ever want another man
 Like you?

Eugene Fitch Ware

The Chaser

by John Collier

Alan Austen, as nervous as a kitten, went up certain dark and creaky stairs in the neighborhood of Pell Street, and peered about for a long time on the dim landing before he found the name he wanted written obscurely on one of the doors.

He pushed open this door, as he had been told to do, and found himself in a tiny room, which contained no furniture but a plain kitchen table, a rocking chair, and an ordinary chair. On one of the dirty buff-colored walls were a couple of shelves, containing in all perhaps a dozen bottles and jars.

An old man sat in the rocking chair, reading a newspaper. Alan, without a word, handed him the card he had been given. "Sit down, Mr. Austen," said the old man very politely. "I am glad to make your acquaintance."

"Is it true," asked Alan, "that you have a certain mixture that has — er — quite extraordinary effects?"

"My dear sir," replied the old man, "my stock in trade is not very large — I don't deal in laxatives and teething mixtures — but such as it is, it is varied. I think nothing I sell has effects which could be precisely described as ordinary."

"Well, the fact is..." began Alan.

"Here, for example," interrupted the old man, reaching for a bottle from the shelf. "Here is a liquid as colorless as water, almost tasteless, quite imperceptible in coffee, wine, or any other beverage. It is also quite imperceptible to any known method of autopsy."

"Do you mean it is a poison?" cried Alan, very much horrified.

"Call it a glove cleaner if you like," said the old man indifferently. "Maybe it will clean gloves. I have never tried. One might call it a life cleaner. Lives need cleaning sometimes."

"I want nothing of that sort," said Alan.

"Probably it is just as well," said the old man. "Do you know the price of this? For one teaspoonful, which is sufficient, I ask 5,000 dollars. Never less. Not a penny less."

"I hope all your mixtures are not as expensive," said Alan apprehensively.

"Oh dear, no," said the old man. "It would be no good charging that sort of price for a love potion, for example. Young people who need a love potion very seldom have 5,000 dollars. Otherwise they would not need a love potion."

"I am glad to hear that," said Alan.

"I look at it like this," said the old man. "Please a customer with one article, and he will come back when he needs another. Even if it *is* more costly. He will save up for it, if necessary."

So," said Alan, "you really do sell love potions?"

"If I did not sell love potions," said the old man, reaching for another bottle, "I should not have mentioned the other matter to you. It is only when one is in a position to oblige that one can afford to be so confidential."

"And these potions," said Alan. "They are not just — just — er — "

"Oh, no," said the old man. "Their effects are permanent, and extend far beyond the mere casual impulse. But they include it. Oh, yes, they include it. Bountifully, insistently. Everlastingly."

"Dear me!" said Alan, attempting a look of scientific detachment. "How very interesting!"

"But consider the spiritual side," said the old man.

"I do, indeed," said Alan.

"For indifference," said the old man, "they substitute devotion. For scorn, adoration. Give one tiny measure of this to the young lady — its flavor is imperceptible in orange juice, soup, or cocktails — and however gay and giddy she is, she will change altogether. She will want nothing but solitude and you."

"I can hardly believe it," said Alan. "She is so fond of parties."

"She will not like them any more," said the old man. "She will be afraid of the pretty girls you may meet."

"She will actually be jealous?" cried Alan in a rapture. "Of me?"

"Yes, she will want to be everything to you."

"She is, already. Only she doesn't care about it."

"She will, when she has taken this. She will care intensely. You will be her sole interest in life."

"Wonderful!" cried Alan.

"She will want to know all you do," said the old man. "All that has happened to you during the day. Every word of it. She will want to know what you are thinking about, why you smile suddenly, why you are looking sad."

"That is love!" cried Alan.

"Yes," said the old man. "How carefully she will

look after you! She will never allow you to be tired, to sit in a draft, to neglect your food. If you are an hour late, she will be terrified. She will think you are killed, or that some siren has caught you."

"I can hardly imagine Diana like that!" cried Alan, overwhelmed with joy.

"You will not have to use your imagination," said the old man. "And, by the way, since there are always sirens, if by any chance you *should*, later on, slip a little, you need not worry. She will forgive you, in the end. She will be terribly hurt, of course, but she will forgive you — in the end."

"That will not happen," said Alan fervently.

"Of course not," said the old man. "But if it did, you need not worry. She would never divorce you. Oh, no! And, of course, she will never give you the least, the very least, grounds for — uneasiness."

"And how much," said Alan, "is this wonderful mixture?"

"It is not as dear," said the old man, "as the glove cleaner, or life cleaner, as I sometimes call it. No. That is 5,000 dollars, never a penny less. One has to be older than you are, to indulge in that sort of thing. One has to save up for it."

"But the love potion?" said Alan.

"Oh, that," said the old man, opening the drawer in the kitchen table, and taking out a tiny, rather dirty-looking vial. "That is just a dollar."

"I can't tell you how grateful I am," said Alan, watching him fill it.

"I like to oblige," said the old man. "Then customers come back, later in life, when they are better off, and want more expensive things. Here you are. You will find it very effective."

"Thank you again," said Alan. "Good-bye."

"Au revoir," said the old man.

I Can't Think What He Sees in Her

Jealousy's an awful thing and foreign to my nature;
I'd punish it by law if I was in the Legislature.
One can't have all of anything, and wanting it is mean,
But still, there is a limit, and I speak of Miss Duveen.

I'm not a jealous woman,
    But I can't see what he sees in her,
        I can't see what he sees in her,
    If she was something striking
    I could understand the liking,
And I wouldn't have a word to say to that;
    But I can't see why he's fond
    Of that objectionable blond —
That fluffy little, stuffy little, flashy little, trashy little,
    creepy-crawly, music-bally, horrid little CAT!

I wouldn't say a word against the girl — be sure of
that;
It's not the creature's fault she has the manners of a
rat.
Her dresses may be dowdy, but her hair is always
new,
And if she squints a little — well, many people do.

   I'm not a jealous woman,
      But I can't see what he sees in her,
         I can't see what he sees in her,
            I can't see what he sees in her!
      He's absolutely free —
      There's no bitterness in me,
Though an ordinary woman would explode;
      I'd only like to know
      What he sees in such a crow
As that insinuating, calculating, irritating, titivating,
   sleepy little, creepy little, sticky little TOAD!

A. P. Herbert

Unfortunate Coincidence

By the time you swear you're his,
  Shivering and sighing,
And he vows his passion is
  Infinite, undying —
Lady, make a note of this:
  One of you is lying.

Dorothy Parker

"Hire him. He's got great legs."

Courtesy of NOW Legal Defense and Education Fund.

From BACK TO B.C. and From HEY! B.C. by Johnny Hart. By permission of John Hart and Field Enterprises, Inc.

From BACK TO B.C. and From HEY! B.C. by Johnny Hart. By permission of John Hart and Field Enterprises, Inc.

A Woman Stops at Nothing

A woman stops at nothing, for nothing's
   shameful, she thinks,
When she rings her neck with emeralds
   and hangs to her ears gold links
With pearls big enough to stretch them.
   Nothing's so hard to endure
As a wealthy woman. Before that, her
   face is foul, each contour
Grotesquely puffed by beauty packs,
   and she reeks and drips
With thick Poppaean creams, which
   stick to her poor husband's lips.
A lover she greets with skin washed
   clean. But when will she care
To look attractive at home? For lovers,
   spikenard's kept there;
For them she buys all that you slender
   Hindus in commerce
Send us. At last she opens her face,
   strips off the first
Of the plasters, and begins to look
   recognizable; then
She's laved in asses' milk, from a herd
   of females, which in
Her train would be led if she were
   banished to the North Pole.
But when she's daubed and treated with
   all those creams and mole

Removers and wrinkle smoothers of
  hot, wet dough, the results are
Questionable: What shall we call it —
  a face or an ulcer?

from Juvenal, Satire VI
Translated by Hubert Creekmore

From BACK TO B.C. and From HEY! B.C. by Johnny Hart. By permission of John Hart and Field Enterprises, Inc.

The Sexes

by Dorothy Parker

The young man with the scenic cravat glanced nervously down the sofa at the girl in the fringed dress. She was examining her handkerchief; it might have been the first one of its kind she had seen, so deep was her interest in its material, form, and possibilities. The young man cleared his throat, without necessity or success, producing a small, syncopated noise.

"Want a cigarette?" he said.

"No, thank you," she said. "Thank you ever so much just the same."

"Sorry I've only got these kind," he said. "You got any of your own?"

"I really don't know," she said. "I probably have, thank you."

"Because if you haven't," he said, "it wouldn't take me a minute to go up to the corner and get you some."

"Oh, thank you, but I wouldn't have you go to all that trouble for anything," she said. "It's awfully sweet of you to think of it. Thank you ever so much."

"Will you for God's sakes stop thanking me?" he said.

"Really," she said, "I didn't know I was saying anything out of the way. I'm awfully sorry if I hurt your feelings. I know what it feels like to get your feelings hurt. I'm sure I didn't realize it was an insult to say 'thank you' to a person. I'm not exactly in the habit of having people swear at me because I say 'thank you' to them."

"I did not swear at you!" he said.

"Oh, you didn't?" she said. "I see."

"My God," he said, "all I said, I simply asked you if I couldn't go out and get you some cigarettes. Is there anything in that to get up in the air about?"

"Who's up in the air?" she said. "I'm sure I didn't know it was a criminal offense to say I wouldn't dream of giving you all that trouble. I'm afraid I must be awfully stupid, or something."

"Do you want me to go out and get you some cigarettes; or don't you?" he said.

"Goodness," she said, "if you want to go so much, please don't feel you have to stay here. I wouldn't have you feel you had to stay for anything."

"Ah, don't be that way, will you?" he said.

"Be what way?" she said. "I'm not being any way."

"What's the matter?" he said.

"Why, nothing," she said. "Why?"

"You've been funny all evening," he said. "Hardly said a word to me, ever since I came in."

"I'm terribly sorry you haven't been having a good time," she said. "For goodness' sakes, don't feel you have to stay here and be bored. I'm sure there are millions of places you could be having a lot more fun. The only thing, I'm a little bit sorry I didn't know before, that's all. When you said you were coming over tonight, I broke a lot of dates to go to the theater and everything. But it doesn't make a bit of difference. I'd much rather have you go and have a good time. It isn't very pleasant to sit here and feel you're boring a person to death."

"I'm not bored!" he said. "I don't want to go any place! Ah, honey, won't you tell me what's the matter? Ah, please."

"I haven't the faintest idea what you're talking about," she said. "There isn't a thing on earth the matter. I don't know what you mean."

"Yes, you do," he said. "There's something the trouble. Is it anything I've done, or anything?"

"Goodness," she said, "I'm sure it isn't any of my business, anything you do. I certainly wouldn't feel I had any right to criticize."

"Will you stop talking like that?" he said. "Will you, please?"

"Talking like what?" she said.

"You know," he said. "That's the way you were talking over the telephone today too. You were so snotty when I called you up, I was afraid to talk to you."

"I beg your pardon," she said. "What did you say I was?"

"Well, I'm sorry," he said. "I didn't mean to say that. You get me so mixed up."

"You see," she said, "I'm really not in the habit of hearing language like that. I've never had a thing like that said to me in my life."

"I told you I was sorry, didn't I?" he said. "Honest, honey, I didn't mean it. I don't know how I came to say a thing like that. Will you excuse me? Please?"

"Oh, certainly," she said. "Goodness, don't feel you have to apologize to me. It doesn't make any difference at all. It just seems a little bit funny to have somebody you were in the habit of thinking was a gentleman come to your home and use language like that to you, that's all. But it doesn't make the slightest bit of difference."

"I guess nothing I say makes any difference to you," he said. "You seem to be sore at me."

"I'm sore at you?" she said. "I can't understand what put that idea in your head. Why should I be sore at you?"

"That's what I'm asking you," he said. "Won't you tell me what I've done? Have I done something to hurt your feelings, honey? The way you were, over the phone, you had me worried all day. I couldn't do a lick of work."

"I certainly wouldn't like to feel," she said, "that I was interfering with your work. I know there are lots of girls that don't think anything of doing things like that, but I think it's terrible. It certainly isn't very nice to sit here and have someone tell you you interfere with his business."

"I didn't say that!" he said. "I didn't say it!"

"Oh, didn't you?" she said. "Well, that was the impression I got. It must be my stupidity."

"I guess maybe I better go," he said. "I can't get right. Everything I say seems to make you sorer and sorer. Would you rather I'd go?"

"Please do just exactly whatever you like," she said. "I'm sure the last thing I want to do is have you stay here when you'd rather be some place else. Why don't you go some place where you won't be bored? Why don't you go up to Florence Leaming's? I know she'd love to have you."

"I don't want to go up to Florence Leaming's!" he said. "What would I want to go up to Florence Leaming's for? She gives me a pain."

"Oh, really?" she said. "She didn't seem to be giving you so much of a pain at Elsie's party last night, I notice. I notice you couldn't even talk to anybody else, that's how much of a pain she gave you."

"Yeah, and you know why I was talking to her?" he said.

"Why, I suppose you think she's attractive," she said. "I suppose some people do. It's perfectly natural. Some people think she's quite pretty."

"I don't know whether she's pretty or not," he said. "I wouldn't know her if I saw her again. Why I was talking to her was you wouldn't even give me a tumble last night. I came up and tried to talk to you, and you just said, 'Oh, how do you do' — just like that, 'Oh, how do you do' — and you turned right away and wouldn't look at me."

"I wouldn't look at you?" she said. "Oh, that's awfully funny. Oh, that's marvelous. You don't mind if I laugh, do you?"

"Go ahead and laugh your head off," he said. "But you wouldn't."

"Well, the minute you came in the room," she said, "you started making such a fuss over Florence Leaming, I thought you never wanted to see anybody else. You two seemed to be having such a wonderful time together, goodness knows I wouldn't have butted in for anything."

"My God," he said, "this what's-her-name girl came up and began talking to me before I even saw anybody else, and what could I do? I couldn't sock her in the nose, could I?"

"I certainly didn't see you try," she said.

"You saw me try to talk to you, didn't you?" he said. "And what did you do? 'Oh, how do you do.' Then this what's-her-name came up again, and there I was, stuck. Florence Leaming! I think she's terrible. Know what I think of her? I think she's a little fool. That's what I think of her."

"Well, of course," she said, "that's the impression she always gave me, but I don't know. I've heard people say she's pretty. Honestly I have."

"Why, she can't be pretty in the same room with you," he said.

"She has got an awfully funny nose," she said. "I really feel sorry for a girl with a nose like that."

"She's got a terrible nose," he said. "You've got a beautiful nose. Gee, you've got a pretty nose."

"Oh, I have not," she said. "You're crazy."

"And beautiful eyes," he said, "and beautiful hair and a beautiful mouth. And beautiful hands. Let me have one of the little hands. Ah, look atta little hand! Who's got the prettiest hands in the world? Who's the sweetest girl in the world?"

"I don't know," she said. "Who?"

"You don't know!" he said. "You do so too know."

"I do not," she said. "Who? Florence Leaming?"

"Oh, Florence Leaming, my eye!" he said. "Getting sore about Florence Leaming! And me not sleeping all last night and not doing a stroke of work all day because you wouldn't speak to me! A girl like you getting sore about a girl like Florence Leaming!"

"I think you're just perfectly crazy," she said. "I was not sore! What on earth ever made you think I was? You're simply crazy. Ow, my new pearl beads! Wait a second till I take them off. There!"

From BOY, GIRL, BOY, GIRL by Jules Feiffer
Copyright © 1959, 1960, 1961 by Jules Feiffer

The Trigamist

by Ivan Krilof

A certain sinner, while his wife was still alive, married two other women secretly. As soon as the news of this reached the king, who was a severe king, and disinclined to permit such scandals, he immediately ordered the polygamist to be tried for the offense, and ordained that such a punishment should be discovered for him as would terrify the whole people, so that no one should in the future be capable of attempting so great a crime. "But if I see that his punishment is a light one," he added, "then I will hang all the judges around the judgment seat."

This pleasantry is disagreeable to the judges. Fear bathes them in a cold sweat. For three whole days they deliberate as to what punishment can be contrived for the culprit. Punishments are plentiful; but experience has proved that none of them will deter people from sinning. However, at last Heaven inspired them. The criminal was brought into court for the announcement of the judicial decision, by which they unanimously decreed —

That he should live with all his three wives at once!

At such a decision the people were lost in astonishment, and expected that the king would hang all the judges. But, before the fifth day arrived, the trigamist had hanged himself.

7. Parody

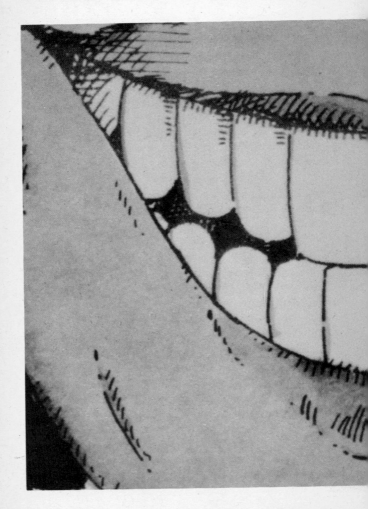

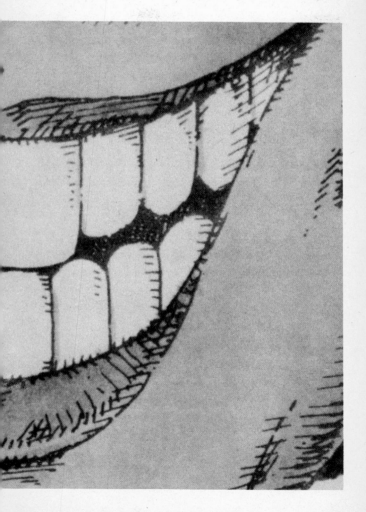

Mary, Mary,
Urban Mary,
How does your sidewalk grow?
With chewing gum wads
With cigarette butts
And popsicle sticks
And potato chip bags
And candy wrappers
And beer cans
And broken bottles
And crusts of pizza
And coffee grounds
And burnt-out light bulbs
And a garbage
    strike all in a row.

from *The Inner City Mother Goose* by Eve Merriam

Now I lay me down to sleep
I pray the double lock will keep;
May no brick through the window break,
And no one rob me till I wake.

There was a crooked man,
And he did very well.

Courtesy of Culver Pictures, Inc.

Fee, fi, fo, fum,
I smell the blood of violence to come;
I smell the smoke that hangs in the air
Of buildings burning everywhere;

Even the rats abandon the city:
The situation is being studied by
    a crisis committee.

In "Endremia and Liason," Robert Benchley comically imitates the stories of the Greek gods and goddesses. The tale parodies both the style and content of the Greek myths.

Endremia and Liason

by Robert C. Benchley

Endremia was the daughter of Polygaminous, the God of Ensilage, and Reba, the Goddess of Licorice. She was the child of a most unhappy union, it later turned out, for when she was a tiny child her father struck her mother with an anvil and turned himself into a lily pad to avoid the vengeance of Jove. But Jove was too sly for Polygaminous and struck him with a bolt of lightning the size of the Merchants Bank Building which threw him completely off his balance so that he toppled over into a chasm and was dashed to death.

In the meantime, Little Endremia found herself alone in the world with nobody but Endrocine, the Goddess of Lettuce, and her son Bilax, the God of Gum Arabic, to look after her. But, as Polygaminous (her father; have you forgotten so soon, you dope?) had turned Endremia into a mushroom before he turned himself into a lily pad, neither of her guardians knew who she was, so their protection did her no good.

But Jove had not so soon forgotten the daughter of his favorite (Reba), and appeared to her one night in the shape of a mushroom gatherer. He asked her how she would like to get off that tree (she was one of those mushrooms which grow on trees) and get into his basket. Endremia, not knowing that it was Jove who was asking her, said not much. Whereupon Jove unloosed his mighty wrath and struck down the whole tree with a bolt of lightning which he had brought with him in case Endremia wouldn't listen to reason.

This is why it is never safe to eat the mushrooms which grow on trees, or to refuse to get into Jove's basket.

From The Complete Tribune Primer

by Eugene Field

*These four parodies imitate the style of primers —
books used to teach children how to read. The content of the orginal primers was usually moralistic,
giving children examples of good manners and conduct.*

The Bad Mamma

Why is this little Girl crying? Because her Mamma
will not let her put Molasses and Feathers on the
Baby's face. What a bad Mamma! The little Girl who
never had any Mamma must enjoy herself. Papas are
Nicer than Mammas. No little Girl ever Marries a
Mamma, and perhaps that is why Mammas are so
Bad to little Girls. Never mind; when Mamma goes
out of the Room, Slap the horrid Baby, and if it
Cries, you can tell your Mamma it Has the Colic.

Generous Richard

This is good Little Richard. His Mamma has Taught him to be Generous. See, he has the Measles, and he is going over to Give them to his Neighbors. Is he not a Nice Boy? When you get the Measles, you must give them to all the little Boys and Girls you can. If you Do, maybe your Mamma will Give you Something. I guess she will Give you a Licking.

The Ink Bottle

Can you See the Ink Bottle on the Table? It is Full of Nice Black Ink. If you Want to, you can Pour the Ink out on the Carpet. It makes the Carpet look Black too, does it not? Sit down on the Carpet and Put both of your Little Paddies in the Ink. See, your Fingers are Covered with Ink. What a Nice picture you can Make on the Wallpaper now. Make a Picture of a Big Man and a Little Girl. Do you want to Put Some Ink on the Lace Curtain? Very well, Put it on Carefully, for you Should never Waste the Ink or anything else. This will be Quite a Surprise to Mamma when she Comes in.

The Foolish Roach

This is a Cock Roach. He is Big, Black, and Ugly. He is Crawling over the Pillow. Do not Say a Word, but lie still and Keep your Mouth open. He will Crawl into Your Mouth and You can Bite him in Two. This will Teach him to be more Discreet in Future.

"Little Andrew" is typical of much of the excessively sentimental poetry written in the late 1800's. Mark Twain makes fun of this style of writing in his parody "Ode to Stephen Dowling Bots, Dec'd."

Little Andrew

Andrew was a little infant,
And his life was two years old;
He was his parents' eldest boy,
And he was drowned, I was told.
His parents never more can see him
In this world of grief and pain,
And Oh! they will not forget him
While on earth they do remain.

On one bright and pleasant morning
His uncle thought it would be nice
To take his dear little nephew
Down to play upon a raft,
Where he was to work upon it,
And this little child would company be —
The raft the water rushed around it,
Yet he the danger did not see.

This little child knew no danger —
Its little soul was free from sin —
He was looking in the water,
When, alas, this child fell in.
Beneath the raft the water took him,
For the current was so strong,
And before they could rescue him
He was drowned and was gone.

Oh! how sad were his kind parents
When they saw their drowned child,
As they brought him from the water,
It almost made their hearts grow wild.
Oh! how mournful was the parting
From that little infant son.
Friends, I pray you, all take warning,
Be careful of your little ones.

Julia A. Moore

Ode to Stephen Dowling Bots, Dec'd

And did young Stephen sicken
   And did young Stephen die?
And did the sad hearts thicken,
   And did the mourners cry?

No; such was not the fate of
   Young Stephen Dowling Bots;
Though sad hearts round him thickened,
   'Twas not from sickness' shots.

No whooping-cough did rack his frame,
   Nor measles drear, with spots;
Not these impaired the sacred name
   Of Stephen Dowling Bots.

Despised love struck not with woe
　　That head of curly knots,
Nor stomach troubles laid him low,
　　Young Stephen Dowling Bots.

Oh no. Then list with tearful eye,
　　Whilst I his fate do tell.
His soul did from this cold world fly,
　　By falling down a well.

They got him out and emptied him;
　　Alas it was too late;
His spirit was gone for to sport aloft
　　In the realms of the good and great.

Mark Twain

The drawings, questions, and answers below are from James Thurber's parody of advice columns, "The Pet Department." Thurber offers tongue-in-cheek advice to distraught pet owners.

Q. Our cat, who is 35, spends all of her time in bed. She follows every move I make, and this is beginning to get to me. She never seems sleepy nor particularly happy. Is there anything I could give her?

MISS L. MC.

A. There are no medicines which can safely be given

to induce felicity in a cat, but you might try lettuce, which is a soporific, for the wakefulness. I would have to see the cat watching you to tell whether anything could be done to divert her attention.

Q. Mr. Jennings bought this beast when it was a pup in Montreal for a St. Bernard, but I don't think it is. It's grown enormously and is stubborn about letting you have anything, like the bath towel it has its paws on, and the hat, both of which belong to Mr. Jennings. He got it that bowling ball to play with but it doesn't seem to like it. Mr. Jennings is greatly attached to the creature.

MRS. FANNY EDWARDS JENNINGS

A. What you have is a bear. While it isn't my bear, I should recommend that you dispose of it. As these animals grow older they get more and more adamant about letting you have anything, until finally there might not be anything in the house you could call your own — except possibly the bowling ball. Zoos use bears. Mr. Jennings could visit it.

Q. The fact that my dog sits this way so often leads me to believe that something is preying on his mind. He seems always to be studying. Would there be any way of finding out what this is?

ARTHUR

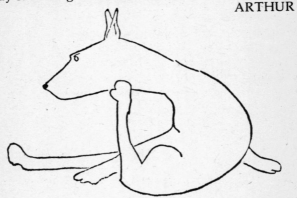

A. Owing to the artificially complex life led by city dogs of the present day, they tend to lose the simpler systems of intuition which once guided all breeds, and frequently lapse into what comes very close to mental perplexity. I myself have known some very profoundly thoughtful dogs. Usually, however, their problems are not serious and I should judge that your dog has merely mislaid something and wonders where he put it.

Q. How would you feel if every time you looked up from your work or anything, there was a horse peering at you from behind something? He prowls about the house at all hours of the day and night. Doesn't seem worried about anything, merely wakeful. What should I do to discourage him?

MRS. GRACE VOYNTON

A. The horse is probably sad. Changing the flowered decorations of your home to something less like open meadows might discourage him, but then I doubt whether it is a good idea to discourage a sad horse. In any case speak to him quietly when he turns up from behind things. Leaping at a horse in a house and crying "Roogie, roogie!" or "Whoosh!" would only result in breakage and bedlam. Of course you might finally get used to having him around, if the house is big enough for both of you.

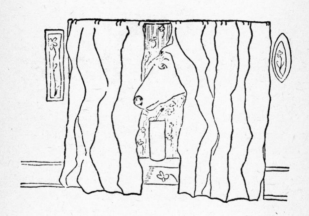

Ovid tells the tragic story of two young lovers, Pyramus and Thisbe, in his poem "Metamorphoses." Shakespeare parodies this story in his play, A Midsummer Night's Dream, turning the lovers' tragic situation into a comic farce.

From "Metamorphoses"

"Pyramus and Thisbe: both the best-looking
Of young people in the East were next-door
Neighbors; they lived within a high-walled, brick-
built
City made (so it was said) by Queen Semiramis.
Proximity was the first reason why
They came to know each other; as time passed
Love flourished, and if their parents had
Not come between them, then they would have
shared
A happy wedding bed. And yet no parent
Can check the heat of love, therefore, the lovers
Burned with mutual flames. Nor friend nor servant
Spoke for them; their speech was in the gesture
Of a nod, a smile; the more they banked the flames
The more they smouldered with a deeper heat.
There was a fissure in the wall between
Their homes, a small thin crevice that no one

Had seen. What eyes are sharper than the eyes
Of love? The lovers found the slit and made it
The hidden mouthpiece of their voices where
Love's subtle words in sweetest whispers came
And charmed the ear. And as they took their places,
Thisbe on one side, Pyramus on his,
Both waited, listening for the other's breath.
'Oh cold and bitter wall,' they said, 'why stand
Between two lovers at your side? Let limbs
And bodies join; at least open your gate
To take our kisses. Yet we do not show
Ingratitude, nor shall we, nor forget
The way through which our words met lovers' ears.'
Divided as they were, each futile day
Was spent in whispers, closing with 'Good night.'
Both pressed their lips against the silent wall.
Next day when dawn outshone the lamps of night
And Sun had dried the dew on frost-white grasses,
The lovers took their places at the wall
And in soft cries complained of heartless fate.
But as they talked they came to a decision:
Under the quiet darkness of the night
To glide from eyes that watched them out-of-doors,
To leave the town behind them; to prevent
The chance of being led astray they chose
The site of Ninus' tomb to meet each other,
There in the shadow of a famous tree,
The white tall mulberry that waved its branches
Not far from a bright flashing stream of water;
The plot delighted them, but from that moment
The day seemed all too long; the quick Sun lagged,
Then dove into the sea where Night came up.

   "No sooner dark than Thisbe, veiled, unseen,
Slipped out-of-doors, a shade among the shadows,
Ran to the tomb, and took her place beneath

The appointed tree. For love had given her
Audacity. But look! A lioness!
And through the moonlit distance Thisbe saw her
With bloody lamb-fed jaws come up the road
And headed toward well waters for a drink
Where through the moonlit distance Thisbe saw her.
The Babylonian girl, trembling yet swift,
Turned to the recess of a darkening cave,
And as she ran dropped her white cloak behind her.
Meanwhile the beast had had her fill of drinking
And as she wandered back between the trees
She stepped across the cloak that Thisbe wore,
Now empty of its mistress, worried it
Between her teeth and left it stained with blood.
A moment later Pyramus arrived
Who saw the footprints of the beast in dust;
Then turned death pale, but when he found the torn
Blood-tinted cloak, he said, 'One night shall be
The killing of two lovers. She whom I love
Deserves the longer life; on me all guilt
Should fall, for it was I who sent her out
Through deepest night into this evil place
Where I arrived too late. May all the lions
Who breed beneath this rocky cliff come at me,
Tear at my body and eat its guilt away —
But only cowards merely ask for death.'
At which he gathered up his Thisbe's cloak
And walked within the shadow of the tree.
There where he kissed the cloak and covered it
With tears. 'Now drink my blood,' he said aloud
And thrust the sword he wore into his side
Then in death's frenzy quickly drew it out.
Torn from warm flesh, and straightway fell
Backward to earth. And as a split lead joint
Shoots hissing sprays of water into air,
So his blood streamed above him to the tree,

Staining white fruit to darkest red, coloring
Tree's roots and growing fruit with purple dye.

"Then Thisbe came from shelter, fearful, shaken,
Thinking perhaps her lover had misplaced her,
Looked for him with her eyes, her soul, her heart,
Trembling to tell him dangers she escaped.
And though she knew the landmarks, the tall tree,
She wondered at the color of its fruit,
Doubting if it was the same tree she saw,
And while she wavered, glanced where something
    moved,
Arms, legs it had, stirring on blood-soaked ground,
Then she stepped back; her face had turned as pale
As the green boxwood leaf, her body tremulous
As fair lake waters rippling in the wind.
But when she saw that it was he, her lover,
She tore her hair and clasped her arms with grief,
Then fondled him, tears poured in wounds and
    blood.
And as she kissed his death-cold lips she cried,
'Pyramus, what misfortune takes you from me?
And oh, Pyramus, speak to answer me.
It is your darling Thisbe calling you.
Listen, my dear, raise up your lazy head.'
At Thisbe's name' Pyramus raised an eyelid,
Weighted with death; her face seen in a vision,
And then his eyes had closed forever more.

"When she discovered her own cloak, the empty
Ivory sheath that held his sword, she said,
'By your own hand even your love has killed you,
Unlucky boy. Like yours my hand has courage,
My heart, love for the last act. I have the strength
To share your death and some shall say I was
The unhappy cause, the partner of your fate;

Only Lord Death had power to take you from me,
Yet even he cannot divorce us now.
Oh twice unhappy parents, his as mine,
Come, take our prayers, nor think the worse of us
Whom true love and death's hour have made one
And we shall sleep in the same bed, our tomb.
And you, oh tree whose branches weave their shad-
     ows
Dark over the pitiful body of one lover
Shall soon bear shade for two; oh fateful tree
Be the memorial of our twin deaths,
And your dark fruit the color of our mourning.'
Then Thisbe placed sword's point beneath her breast
The blade still warm with blood from her love's
     heart,
And leaned upon it till she sank to earth.
Her prayers had reached the gods, had moved both
     parents:
The ripe fruit of the tree turned deep rose color;
And they who loved sleep in a single turn."

Ovid
Translated by M. Gregory

From
A Midsummer
Night's Dream

by William Shakespeare

(*Flourish of trumpets. Enter* QUINCE *for the*
PROLOGUE.)

PROL. If[1] we offend, it is with our goodwill.
That you should think, we come not to offend,
But with goodwill. To show our simple skill,
That is the true beginning of our end.
Consider then, we come but in despite.[2]
We do not come, as minding to content you,
Our true intent is. All for your delight,
We are not here. That you should here repent you,
The actors are at hand, and, by their show,
You shall know all, that you are like to know.

(*Enter* PYRAMUS *and* THISBE, WALL,
MOONSHINE, *and* LION.)

PROL. Gentles, perchance you wonder at this
show,
But wonder on, till truth make all things plain.
This man is Pyramus, if you would know.
This beauteous lady Thisby is certain.
This man, with lime and roughcast, doth present
Wall, that vile Wall which did these lovers sunder,
And through Wall's chink, poor souls, they are content

1 *If... know:* Quince, by mistaking his punctuation, makes
woeful sense of his words. 2 *despite:* ill will.

To whisper. At the which let no man wonder.
This man, with lanthorn,[3] dog, and bush of thorn,
Presenteth Moonshine; for, if you will know,
By moonshine did these lovers think no scorn
To meet at Ninus' tomb, there, there to woo.
This grisly beast, which Lion hight[4] by name,
The trusty Thisby, coming first by night,
Did scare away, or rather did affright.
And, as she fled, her mantle she did fall,[5]
Which Lion vile with bloody mouth did stain.
Anon comes Pyramus, sweet youth and tall,
And finds his trusty Thisby's mantle slain.
Whereat, with blade, with bloody blameful blade,
He bravely broached his boiling bloody breast.
And Thisby, tarrying in mulberry shade,
His dagger drew, and died. For all the rest,
Let Lion, Moonshine, Wall, and lovers twain
At large discourse, while here they do remain.
    (*Exeunt* PROLOGUE, PYRAMUS, THISBE,
    LION, *and* MOONSHINE.)
WALL. In this same interlude it doth befall
That I, one Snout by name, present a wall,
And such a wall, as I would have you think,
That had in it a crannied[6] hole or chink,
Through which the lovers, Pyramus and Thisby,
Did whisper often very secretly.
This loam, this roughcast, and this stone doth show
That I am that same wall. The truth is so.
And this the cranny is, right and sinister,[7]
Through which the fearful lovers are to whisper.
    (*Reenter* PYRAMUS.)
PYR. Oh grim-looked night! Oh night with hue so
    black!
Oh night, which ever art when day is not!
Oh night, Oh night! alack, alack, alack,
    I fear my Thisby's promise is forgot!
And thou, Oh wall, Oh sweet, Oh lovely wall,
    That stand'st between her father's ground and
    mine!
Thou wall, Oh wall, oh sweet and lovely wall,
    Show me thy chink, to blink through with mine
    eyne!
    (WALL *holds up his fingers.*)
        3 *Lanthorn:* lantern with horn sides. 4 *hight:* called. 5 *fall:*
        let fall. 6 *crannied:* cracked. 7 *sinister:* left handed.
220

Thanks, courteous wall. Jove shield thee well for this!
  But what see I? No Thisby do I see.
Oh wicked wall, through whom I see no bliss!
  Cursed be thy stones for thus deceiving me!
  (*Reenter* THISBE.)
THIS. Oh wall, full often hast thou heard my moans,
  For parting my fair Pyramus and me!
My cherry lips have often kissed thy stones,
  Thy stones with lime and hair knit up in thee.
PYR. I see a voice. Now will I to the chink,
To spy an I can hear my Thisby's face.
Thisby!
  THIS. My love thou art, my love I think.
  PYR. Think what thou wilt, I am thy lover's grace;
And, like Limander,[8] am I trusty still.
  THIS. And I like Helen,[9] till the Fates me kill.
  PYR. Not Shafalus to Procrus[10] was so true.
  THIS. As Shafalus to Procrus, I to you.
  PYR. Oh, kiss me through the hole of this vile wall!
  THIS. I kiss the wall's hole, not your lips at all.
  PYR. Wilt thou at Ninny's tomb meet me straightway?
  THIS. 'Tide life, 'tide death, I come without delay.
    (*Exeunt* PYRAMUS *and* THISBE.)
  WALL. Thus have I, wall, my part discharged so;
And, being done, thus wall away doth go. (*Exit.*)
    (*Reenter* LION *and* MOONSHINE.)
  LION. You, ladies, you, whose gentle hearts do fear
  The smallest monstrous mouse that creeps on floor,
May now perchance both quake and tremble here,
  When lion rough in wildest rage doth roar.
Then know that I, one Snug the joiner, am
A lion fell,[11] nor else no lion's dam;
For, if I should as lion come in strife
Into this place, 'twere pity on my life.[12]
  MOON. This lanthorn doth the hornèd moon present,
Myself the man i' the moon do seem to be. This
thornbush is my thornbush; and this dog, my dog.

8 *Limander:* for "Leander." 9 *Helen:* for "Hero," Leander's
love. 10 *Shafalus to Procrus:* Cephalus to Procris. 11 *fell:*
fierce. 12 *pity...life:* i.e., I should be hanged for it.

(*Reenter* THISBE.)

THIS. This is old Ninny's tomb. Where is my love?

LION. (*Roaring*) Oh — (THISBE *runs off.*)

(*Reenter* PYRAMUS.)

PYR. Sweet Moon, I thank thee for thy sunny beams,
I thank thee, Moon, for shining now so bright.
For, by thy gracious, golden, glittering gleams,
I trust to take of truest Thisby sight.
    But stay, oh, spite!
    But mark, poor knight,
What dredful dole[13] is here!
    Eyes, do you see?
    How can it be?
Oh, dainty duck! Oh, dear!
    Thy mantle good,
    What, stained with blood!
Approach, ye Furies fell!
    Oh Fates, come, come,
    Cut thread and thrum,[14]
Quail,[15] crush, conclude, and quell![16]

PYR. Oh wherefore, Nature, didst thou lions frame?
Since lion vile hath here deflowered my dear,
Which is —'no, no — which was the fairest dame
That lived, that loved, that liked, that looked with cheer.
    Come, tears, confound.
    Out, sword, and wound
The pap of Pyramus.
    Aye, that left pap,
    Where heart doth hop. (*Stabs himself.*)
Thus die I, thus, thus, thus.
    Now am I dead,
    Now am I fled,
My soul is in the sky.
    Tongue, lose thy light,
    Moon, take thy flight, (*Exit moonshine.*)
Now die, die, die, die. (*Dies.*)

(*Reenter* THISBE.)

THIS. Asleep, my love?
    What, dead, my dove?

13 *dole:* dolor, grief. 14 *thrum:* lit., the end of the thread in a
piece of weaving. So *cut thread and thrum* means "destroy
everything." 15 *Quail:* overwhelm. 16 *quell:* slay.

Oh Pyramus, arise!
Speak, speak. Quite dumb?
Dead, dead? A tomb
Must cover thy sweet eyes.
These lily lips,
This cherry nose,
These yellow cowslip cheeks,
Are gone, are gone.
Lovers, make moan.
His eyes were green as leeks.
Oh Sisters Three,[17]
Come, come to me,
With hands as pale as milk,
Lay them in gore,
Since you have shore
With shears his thread of silk.
Tongue, not a word.
Come, trusty sword,
Come, blade, my breast imbrue.[18]
(*Stabs herself.*)
And, farewell, friends.
Thus Thisby ends.
Adieu, adieu, adieu. (*Dies.*)

17 *Sisters Three*: the three Fates who sit spinning man's destiny. 18 *imbrue*: make bloody.

"Mona Gorilla" by Rick Meyerowitz